Finding Needles in a Haystack

Keywords for Finding Top Talent in Resume Databases

Volume III

Wendy S. Enelow, CCM, MRW, JCTC, CPRW

© 2009 Wendy S. Enelow
All Rights Reserved.
Printed in the United States of America.

ISBN: 1-928734-53-7

Special discounts on bulk quantities of WEDDLE's books are available for libraries, corporations, professional associations and other organizations. For details, please contact WEDDLE's at 203.964.1888.

This publication may not be reproduced, stored in a retrieval system or transmitted, in whole or part, in any form or by any means, electronic, mechanical, photocopying, recording or otherwise, without the prior written permission of WEDDLE's, 2052 Shippan Avenue, Stamford, CT 06902.

WEDDLE's
www.weddles.com
2052 Shippan Avenue
Stamford, CT 06902

Where People Matter Most

About the Author

Wendy Enelow is widely regarded as one of the leading resume writers in the world. Over her more than 20-year career, she has helped thousands of individuals craft their resumes with the clarity and exactitude necessary to position them for the right openings with the right employers. Her resumes open doors and help to generate opportunities.

Wendy has been published, featured, and/or quoted in numerous publications including *Time Magazine*, *The Wall Street Journal*, *The New York Times*, and countless others. In addition, her articles have appeared on hundreds of career-related websites, including TheLadders, CareerJournal. Monster, and NETSHARE. Currently she is the featured careers columnist for *The American Legion Magazine*.

Wendy is the founder and past president of the Career Masters Institute, a professional association for career coaches, career counselors, resume writers, outplacement consultants, and other career management professionals. She is a graduate of the University of Maryland and has earned an impressive array of employment-related credentials, including:

- Master Resume Writer (MRW),
- Certified Professional Resume Writer (CPRW),
- Job and Career Transition Coach (JCTC), and
- Credentialed Career Master (CCM).

Wendy is the author of numerous resume and job search books. Among her titles are:

- *Enelow-Kusmark Executive Resume Toolkit*
- *Executive Job Search for $100K to $1 Million+ Jobs*
- *Best Resumes For $100,000+ Jobs*
- *Best Career Transition Resumes For $100,000+ Jobs*
- *Best Resumes For College Grads To Land $75,000+ Jobs*
- *Best Resumes For People Without A Four-Year Degree*
- *Best Resumes & CVs For International Jobs*
- *KeyWords To Nail Your Job Interview*

- *Best Keywords for Resumes, Cover Letters & Interviews*
- *Expert Resumes for Engineering Professionals*
- *Expert Resumes For Managers & Executives*
- *Expert Resumes For Web & Computer Professionals*
- *Expert Resumes for Teachers & Educators*
- *Expert Resumes For Career Changers*
- *Expert Resumes For People Returning To Work*
- *Expert Resumes for Military-to-Civilian Transitions*
- *Expert Resumes For Manufacturing Industry Professionals*
- *The $100,000+ Entrepreneur*

Table of Contents

Introduction	*Optimizing Your Keyword Searches for Resumes*	i
Chapter 1	*Accounting, Auditing, Bookkeeping & Collections*	1
Chapter 2	*Administration, Office Management & Secretarial Services*	21
Chapter 3	*Advertising & Corporate Communications*	39
Chapter 4	*Architecture*	53
Chapter 5	*Art & Design*	77
Chapter 6	*Customer Service*	97
Chapter 7	*Equipment Installation, Maintenance & Repair*	109
Chapter 8	*Hazardous Materials*	175
Chapter 9	*Manufacturing & Production Operations*	185
Chapter 10	*Public Relations & Public Affairs*	291
Chapter 11	*Purchasing*	305
Chapter 12	*Security*	317
Chapter 13	*Translation & Interpretation*	327
Chapter 14	*Transportation, Logistics, Warehousing & Distribution*	337
Chapter 15	*Writing, Editing & Journalism*	385

Appendix A	*Action Verbs*	397
Appendix B	*Personality Descriptors*	403
Appendix C	*General Skills, Qualifications & Attributes*	407

Introduction

Optimizing Your Keyword Searches for Resumes

Finding the best candidates for your recruiting requirements is an increasingly complex and demanding challenge. There are millions of resumes posted on tens of thousands of sites on the Internet and probably as many stored in corporate and staffing firm resume management systems. They undoubtedly include the best prospects for each of your openings, and yet, they are virtually invisible. You can't access them unless you can find them in the online and computerized databases in which they are archived. And, that's what keywords can do for you.

Keywords enable you to probe the resumes that are stored both on the Web and in your own resume management system. They detail the criteria—the specific qualifications for which you're searching in a candidate's record—that you must use with:

- Search engines such as Google, MSN and Yahoo!;
- The resume databases on job boards such as Monster, CareerBuilder.com, Dice, and VetJobs; and
- The computer that operates your resume management system.

Wherever it's done, searching for resumes with keywords is a fairly straightforward proposition. For example, if you enter the keywords *pharmaceutical*, *key account management*, and *product launch* into a search engine or computer, every resume with one or more of those words in it will be selected. It's that easy. The only challenge is:

Where do you find the right keywords for each of the positions you're trying to fill?

Fortunately, you're holding that resource right in your hands!

Finding Needles in a Haystack

Finding Needles In A Haystack is the first-ever, comprehensive, keyword reference book for corporate and third party recruiters, HR professionals with recruiting responsibilities and researchers working with executive search consultants. This 3-volume series provides more than 25,000 keywords and keyword phrases for more than 5400 different job titles representing all major industries and professions.

In this, the third volume in the series, you'll find critical keywords and keyword phrases for the following career fields:

- Accounting, Auditing, Bookkeeping & Collections
- Administration, Office Management & Secretarial Services
- Advertising & Corporate Communications
- Architecture
- Art & Design
- Customer Service
- Equipment Installation, Maintenance & Repair
- Hazardous Materials
- Manufacturing & Production Operations
- Public Relations & Public Affairs
- Purchasing
- Security
- Translation & Interpretation
- Transportation, Logistics, Warehousing & Distribution
- Writing, Editing & Journalism
- Appendix A: Action Verbs
- Appendix B: Personality Descriptors
- Appendix C: General Skills, Qualifications & Attributes

The other two volumes of the series cover the following career fields and topics:

Volume I

- Engineering
- Executive Management, General Management & C-Level Positions
- Finance & Economics

Introduction

- Health Care
- Human Resources
- Sales & Marketing
- Technology
- Appendix A: Action Verbs
- Appendix B: Personality Descriptors
- Appendix C: General Skills, Qualifications & Attributes

Volume II

- Banking
- Broadcasting & Media
- Construction
- Dentistry
- Food & Beverage
- Hospitality
- Insurance
- Investment Finance
- Law
- Pharmacy
- Psychology & Counseling
- Real Estate
- Retail
- Science
- Social Work, Social Services & Human Services
- Teaching & Education
- Appendix A: Action Verbs
- Appendix B: Personality Descriptors
- Appendix C: General Skills, Qualifications & Attributes

How to Use This Book

To use this book wisely and effectively, you must understand its structure and layout. That knowledge will enable you to optimize your online search results.

Each chapter in each volume has the same basic format for each career field:
- Representative Job Titles
- Software, Systems & Technology
- Keywords & Keyword Phrases
- Additional Keywords & Keyword Phrases (for professional specializations)

Here's an example:

If you're doing a search for a Chemical Engineer, go to the Engineering career field chapter to find the extensive list of keywords and keyword phrases for the Engineering profession in general. Start by reviewing that list and identifying all of the keywords that are relevant to the particular position for which you're recruiting.

Then, proceed to the subheading of Chemical Engineering where you'll find additional keywords and keyword phrases that are specific to Chemical Engineering and not to other Engineering disciplines. That list is even more critical as it is a more definitive and finite representation of the skills, qualifications, technical competencies, and other factors required of the "typical" Chemical Engineer.

Combine the general Engineering and the Chemical Engineering keywords and keyword phrases together, and you're now ready to conduct a quick and efficient online search for candidates whose qualifications match the requirements of your specific opening.

If certain personality traits will also be important in determining the best candidate for the position, you can supplement the career field keywords with personality descriptors from Appendix B and general skills and qualifications from Appendix C. Then, if your final list of keywords is too long, delete some

Introduction

of the more general keywords and focus on the words that are most closely related to the Chemical Engineering field and to the specific requirements and responsibilities of each position you are working to fill.

There are several other critical elements to consider in order to optimize your use of this book:

- ◆ Job titles are keywords and can be used in your resume searches. Refer to the Representative Job Titles section at the beginning of each chapter for a listing of titles that may be appropriate to a particular opening, even if it is not the specific title your organization or client uses.

- ◆ Acronyms are also keywords and are appropriate for inclusion in your resume searches. Throughout this series, you'll find many listings where both the word and the acronym are listed together. For example, in the Customer Service Chapter in Volume III, you'll find the following keyword phrase - *Customer Relationship Management (CRM)*. Both *Customer Relationship Management* and *CRM* are used interchangeably on candidate resumes, so be certain to use both in your searches.

- ◆ Software, systems, and technology terms are sometimes keywords, and they too can be used in your resume searches. Refer to that section in each chapter to identify the appropriate technology keywords and keyword phrases you need for each of your specific openings.

- ◆ Most keywords are listed in their singular rather than their plural form. However, there are instances when the plural form of a word is provided. The determining factor for deciding which form should be included in this book – whether singular or plural - was the most common usage of the word.

- ◆ Hyphenation was a complex issue to deal with in this book as many keyword phrases would typically include a hyphen between two words. Since hyphens can sometimes throw off a search engine or computer, they are rarely included in any of the keyword lists and only when absolutely necessary.

- ◆ Multiple uses of the same word root have been provided throughout the book to give you keyword options that are as comprehensive as possible and to provide you with all commonly used forms of that word. For example, in the Sales & Marketing Chapter, you'll find both *Sales Manager* and *Sales Management*.

An alternative approach is to use truncation, which most search engines now permit. Simply put, truncation is the process of using a searchable shortened form of a keyword. You could, for example, enter *Sales Manag** into a search engine and all words that begin with *Manag* will be displayed. This technique provides you with the convenience of being able to capture related keywords and keyword phrases with just a few keystrokes.

One word of caution: Some search engines use the asterisk symbol (*), while others use the question mark (?) for truncated search terms. Google, on the other hand, works with both. You'll need to experiment with the search engine you're using to see which symbol it will accept.

Truncation can also be extremely helpful in identifying alternative spellings of the same word. Using all potential spellings of a word has become an especially critical consideration as the Internet and online resume search now spans the globe. You are likely, as a result, to encounter a variety of spellings for the same word (e.g., flavor or flavour), and truncation (i.e., using *flavo*r* or *flavo?r* as your keyword) will ensure that you capture all of the resumes with any of these variations.

◆ In each chapter, you'll also find that space has been provided for you to record additional or new keywords and keyword phrases. Keywords are dynamic and constantly changing as occupational terminology evolves. Although the keyword lists in this book are as comprehensive as possible, there will be instances where you'll want to add your own keywords and keyword phrases. The space provided in each chapter is precisely for that use.

With *Finding Needles In A Haystack* in hand, you'll be able to tackle resume search, both online and off, with ease and confidence. You can now quickly identify the top candidates for your openings, build your talent pipeline for your current and future staffing needs, and accelerate the success of your recruiting efforts.

Finding Needles in a Haystack

Keywords for Finding Top Talent in Resume Databases

Finding Needles in a Haystack

Chapter 1

Accounting, Auditing, Bookeeping & Collections

Principal Keyword List:

Accounting, Auditing, Bookkeeping & Collections

Additional Keyword Lists:

Auditing
Collections

Representative Job Titles

Account Collector
Account Resolution Analyst
Account Resolution Clerk
Accountant
Accounting Analyst
Accounting Assistant
Accounting Associate
Accounting Clerk
Accounting Manager
Accounting Representative
Accounting Specialist
Accounting Supervisor
Accounting Technician
Accounts Payable Clerk
Accounts Receivable Clerk
Accredited Business Accountant (ABA)
Accredited Tax Advisor (ATA)
Accredited Tax Preparer (ATP)
Analyst
Appraiser
Assistant Bookkeeper
Assistant Controller
Audit Manager
Auditing Clerk
Auditor
Auditor-in-Charge
Bill Collector
Billing Clerk
Billing Manager
Bookkeeper
Bookkeeping Clerk
Budget Analyst
Business Analyst
Cash Accountant
Certified Cash Manager (CCM)
Certified Financial Services Auditor (CFSA)
Certified Internal Auditor (CIA)

Accounting, Auditing, Bookeeping & Collections

Certified Management Accountant (CMA)
Certified Public Accountant (CPA)
Chief Accounting Officer (CAO)
Chief Administrative Officer (CAO)
Claims Adjuster
Coding Clerk
Collections Clerk
Collections Manager
Collector
Compliance Analyst
Comptroller
Controller
Corporate Comptroller
Corporate Controller
Cost Accountant
Cost Analyst
Cost Estimator
Cost Manager
Credit Administrator
Credit Analyst
Credit Clerk
Credit Collections Clerk
Credit Collections Manager
Credit Manager
Debt Collector
External Auditor
Financial Accountant
Financial Analyst
Financial Auditor
Fiscal Technician
Forensic Accountant
General Accountant
General Ledger Accountant
Internal Auditor
Junior Accountant
Management Accountant
Mathematical Technician
Mathematician
Operational Risk Analyst

Operations Research Analyst
Partnership Accountant
Project Accountant
Public Accountant
Relationship Manager
Research Analyst
Revenue Agent
Risk Manager
Senior Accountant
Senior Auditor
Staff Accountant
Staff Analyst
Telephone Collector

Accounting, Auditing, Bookeeping & Collections

Software, Systems & Technology

4n6xprt Systems StiffCalcs
Accountants Template JAZZ-It!
ACCUCert
Accutrac
AcornSystems Corporate Performance Management
ACT!
ADP EasyPay
ADP/Vantra VOLTS
ADS Advantage
Adtec Agency Manager
Agency Management Systems (AMS 360)
Allied Financial Software Act4Advisors
Anodas Software Limited Phoenix
AppleWorks
ARES Corporation PRISM Project Estimator
ARSoftware WinSMAC
atGlobal Allegro
atGlobal webMBR
AuditWare
Austin Logistics CallSelect
Axonwave Fraud & Abuse Management System
BCCORP Burkitt W5
BCCORP W5
Benefits Technology Group SalesLogix
BizBench Benchmarking Software
Bloomberg Professional
BLS Software Invoice!
BusinessObjects Desktop Intelligence
Cartesis ES Magnitude
CCC EzNet
CCH ProSystem
CGI-AMS BureauLink Enterprise
CGI-AMS CACS Enterprise
Cognos 8 Business Intelligence
Columbia Ultimate Remit
Consilience Software Maven Insurance Automation Suite

Corel QuattroPro
Corporate Responsibility System Technologies Limited (CRSTL)
Compliance Posting System
Credit Adjudication & Lending Management System (CALMS)
CSC Automated Work Distributor (AWD)
CSI Complex Systems ClientTrade
Cygnus Software IncomeMax
dailyVest Investment Personalization Platform
Deltek Costpoint
Derivicom FinOptions XL
Enterprise Resource Planning (ERP)
Equifax Application Engine
Experian Credinomics
Experian Strategy Management
Experian Transact SM
Fair Isaac Claims Advisor
FileMaker Pro
FileNet Content Manager
Financeware Finance File Manager
FiServ Advanced Underwriting Software
FlexiLedger
FLS eDP Payrolltax
FRx
FundCount Web
General Examination System (GENESYS)
Hyperion Business Performance Management Suite
Hyperion Enterprise
Hyperion Pillar
IBM Check Processing Control System (CPCS)
IBM Lotus 1-2-3
IBM Lotus Notes
Imagine Trading System
Injury Sciences EDR Insight
Insurance Technologies ForeSight Enterprise
InSystems Calligo Document Management System
Intrax ProcedureNet
Intuit QuickBooks
Ivorix Neurostrategy Finance
LabOne NET

Accounting, Auditing, Bookeeping & Collections

Leading Market Technologies EXPO
LexisNexis Banko
LexisNexis RiskWise
Lotus 1-2-3
Lotus Notes
Lumigent Entegra
Magnify Predictive Targeting System
Matheny Pattern Forecaster Plus
Mathworks MATLAB
MethodWare ProAudit Advisor
Microsoft Access
Microsoft Excel
Microsoft Great Plains
Microsoft Outlook
Microsoft PowerPoint
Microsoft Project
Microsoft Visual FoxPro
Microsoft Word
MoneyTree Silver Financial Planner
Moody's KMV FAMAS
Moody's KMV Risk Advisor
Moody's KMV Risk Analyst
Neural Network Modeling
NeuroSolutions
NeuroSolutions for MATLAB
NILS INSource
Novell GroupWise
OmniRIM
Online Analytical Processing (OLAP)
Oracle
Oracle Corporate Performance Management (CPM)
Oracle Financials
Oracle PeopleSoft
Oversight Systems
Paisley Cardmap
Pentana Audit Work System (PAWS)
PhotoModeler
PriceWaterhouseCoopers TeamMate
ProxyEdge

Quantrax Intelec
Realm Business Solutions INSIGHT for ARGUS
Redtail
RGA Facultative Application Console
Sage CPAClient Checkbook
Sage CPAPractice Manager
Sage Fixed Asset Solution
Sage MAS 200 ERP
Sage MAS 90 ERP
Sage MIP Fund Accounting
Sage Software Accpac ERP
SAP
SAP Business One
Satori Group proCube
ScanSoft PaperPort Pro
SIS SEMCI Partner
Skyware Software InsBridge
Solomon
S-PLUS
SPSS
SS&C PTS
St. Paul Travelers e-CARMA
Star Software Materiality Calculator
StrataCare StrataWare eReview
Structured Query Language (SQL)
SunGard LockBox
SunGard MicroHedge
Sync Essentials Trade Accountant
System for Electronic Rate & Form Filing (SERFF)
System Innovators Software
Tangle S Creations Your Insurance Office
TCI XML Credit Interface
The Agency Advantage
Thomson GoSystem Tax
Tillinghast Actuarial Software (TAS)
TradeTools Financial Market Database
TradeTools Monthly U.S. Economic Database
Trading Blox
TrendTracker Compliance Solution

Accounting, Auditing, Bookeeping & Collections

Tropics
Tropics Claims Reserve Management
Turtle Creek Software Goldenseal Architect
United Systems & Software Individual Life & Health Administration System
Universal Tax Systems TaxWise
Valen Technologies Risk Manager
Valiant Vantage
Visual FoxPro
Visual Statement Investigator Suite
Vulcan Solutions
W3 Data BatchAppend411
Ward Systems Group GeneHunter
Ward Systems Group NeuralShell Predictor
Ward Systems Group NeuroShell Trader
WealthTec Foundations
WeathTec WealthMaster
Web Information Solutions Pocket Informant
Westlaw
Wolfram Research Mathematica
Wolfram Research Mathematica Financial Essentials
Wolfram Research Mathematica Pricing Engine
Workforce Time & Attendance
WORLDOX

KeyWords & KeyWord Phrases for Accounting, Auditing, Bookkeeping & Collections

Account
Account Coding
Account Invoice
Account Posting
Account Statements
Accounting
Accounting Journals
Accounting Practices
Accounting Principles
Accounting Recordkeeping
Accounting Records
Accounting Reports
Accounting System
Accounting Tables
Accounts Payable
Accounts Receivable
Accreditation Council for Accountancy & Taxation (ACAT)
Accrual Accounting
Algebra
American Accounting Association (AAA)
American Institute of Certified Public Accountants (AICPA)
Annual Budget
Appropriations
Arithmetic
Asset Allocation
Asset Disposition
Assets
Balance Sheet
Bank
Banking
Bill
Billing
Bookkeeping
Budget
Budget Administration

Accounting, Auditing, Bookeeping & Collections

Budget Analysis
Budget Development
Budget Estimates
Budget Forecasting
Budget Planning
Budget Preparation
Budgeted Costs
Budgeting
Business Forecasting
Business Transactions
Calculations
Calculus
Canadian Institute of Chartered Accountants (CICA)
Capital Budget
Capital Expenditures
Cash
Cash Accounting
Cash Flow Management
Cash Flow Projections
Cash Management
Cash Receipts
Cash Reconciliation
Chartered Institute of Management Accountants (CIMA)
Charts
Claims Adjustment
Claims Administration
Claims Investigation
Claims Settlement
Client Management
Coding
Commercial Banking
Compliance
Corporate Administration
Corporate Finance
Corporate Reporting
Cost Accounting
Cost Analysis
Cost Avoidance
Cost Estimating

Cost Management
Cost Reduction
Cost-Benefit Analysis
Costs
Data
Data Analysis
Data Collection
Data Integrity
Debit
Debt
Debt Financing
Departmental Budgeting
Earnings Before Interest & Taxes (EBIT)
Earnings Before Interest Depreciation Taxes and Amortization (EBITDA)
Earnings Forecast
Economic Analysis
Economic Forecasting
Economic Performance
Economic Practices
Economic Principles
Economic Theory
Economics
Electronic Financial Services
Enterprise Resource Planning (ERP)
Expenditure Control
Expenditures
Expense Budget
Expense Control
Expenses
Feasibility Analysis
Finance
Financial Accounting
Financial Analysis
Financial Budget
Financial Controls
Financial Data
Financial Examination
Financial Forecasting
Financial Instruments

Accounting, Auditing, Bookeeping & Collections

Financial Management
Financial Markets
Financial Models
Financial Planning
Financial Plans
Financial Recordkeeping
Financial Records
Financial Regulations
Financial Reporting
Financial Reserves
Financial Resources
Financial Services
Financial Statements
Financial Strategies
Financial Transactions
Fiscal
Fiscal Allocation
Fixed Assets
Forecasting
Forensic Accounting
Fraud
Funds Accounting
Funds Management
General Accounting
General Ledger
General Ledger Accounting
Generally Accepted Accounting Principles (GAAP)
Governmental Accounting
Graphs
Income
Income Statement
Income Verification
Information Systems
Information Technology
Institute of Management Accountants (IMA)
Internal Revenue Service (IRS)
Invoice
Invoicing
Job Costing

Journal Records
Journals
Ledger
Ledger Sheets
Legal Compliance
Legal Review
Letters of Credit
Liabilities
Line of Credit
Make/Buy Analysis
Management Accounting
Margin Improvement
Mathematical Accuracy
Mathematics
Mathematics Reasoning
National Association of State Boards of Accountancy (NASBA)
National Association of State Budget Officers (NASBO)
National Society of Certified Public Accountants (NSCPA)
Non-Compliance
Notes Payable
Notes Receivable
Numerical Data
Operating Budget
Operating Costs
Operating Expenses
Operating Income
Operations Research
Overhead Expenses
Partnership Accounting
Policies & Procedures
Product Pricing
Product Pricing Analysis
Profit & Loss (P&L)
Profit & Loss (P&L) Reporting
Profit & Loss (P&L) Statement
Profit Gains
Profitability Analysis
Project Accounting
Project Financing

Accounting, Auditing, Bookeeping & Collections

Project Management
Public Accounting
Public Records
Receipt Books
Receipts
Receivables
Regulations
Regulatory Affairs
Regulatory Compliance
Regulatory Reporting
Regulatory Standards
Relationship Management
Research
Research Analysis
Reserves
Resource Utilization
Return on Assets (ROA)
Return on Equity (ROE)
Return on Investment (ROI)
Revenue
Revenue Gain
Service Pricing
Service Pricing Analysis
Shareholder Reporting
Shareholders
Sound Financial Policies
Spreadsheets
Staff Accounting
Standards
Statistical Analysis
Statistical Procedures
Statistical Reporting
Statistics
Stockholder Reporting
Strategic Planning
Tax
Tax Analysis
Tax Laws
Tax Liability

Tax Planning
Tax Preparation
Tax Regulations
Tax Return
Tax Shelter
Tax Strategies
Team Building
Team Leadership
Training & Development
Transactions
Trust
Trust Accounting
Valuation
Workpapers

Accounting, Auditing, Bookeeping & Collections

Additional Keywords & Keyword Phrases for Auditing

Accounting Audit
Audit
Audit Controls
Audit Findings
Audit Management
Audit Report
Audit Reporting
Audit Tables
Audit Workpapers
Auditing
External Audit
Financial Audit
Information Systems Audit & Control Association (ISACA)
Institute of Internal Auditors (IIA)
Internal Audit
Internal Controls
Inventory Audit
Management Audit
Materials Audit
Merchandise Audit
Operational Audit
Operational Risk Analysis
Operations Audit
Risk
Risk Analysis
Risk Assessment
Risk Controls
Risk Management
Risk Spread
Supply Audit
Systems Audit
Technology Audit

Additional Keywords & Keyword Phrases for Collections

Account Collections
Account Delinquency
Account Resolution
Account Status
Autodialer
Bill
Bill Collections
Billing
Collections
Collections Management
Collections Recovery
Contract Review
Contract Terms & Conditions
Credit
Credit & Collections
Credit Accounts
Credit Analysis
Credit Department
Credit Line
Credit Management
Credit Ratings & Ceilings
Credit Review
Credit Terms & Conditions
Credit Transaction
Damage Claim
Debt
Debt Collections
Debt Repayment
Delinquency
Delinquent Account
Invoices
Mail Collections
Merchandise Return
On-Site Collections
Overdue Account
Overdue Payment

Accounting, Auditing, Bookeeping & Collections

Past Due Accounts
Payment Collection
Payment Posting
Payment Processing
Payment Solicitation
Payment Statement
Payments
Predictive Dialer
Product Returns
Receipt Book
Repayment
Repayment Schedule
Repossession
Repossession Proceedings
Statement
Telephone Collections

Add Your Own Keywords & Keyword Phrases

Chapter 2

Administration, Office Management & Secretarial Services

Principal Keyword List:

Accounting, Auditing, Bookkeeping & Collections

Additional Keyword Lists:

Legal Secretarial Services
Medical Secretarial Services

Representative Job Titles

Administrative Assistant
Accredited Legal Secretary (ALS)
Administrative Aide
Administrative Assistant
Administrative Associate
Administrative Coordinator
Administrative Director
Administrative Manager
Administrative Office Manager
Administrative Officer
Administrative Secretary
Administrative Services Assistant
Administrative Services Associate
Administrative Services Manager
Administrative Services Supervisor
Administrative Specialist
Administrative Supervisor
Administrative Support Assistant
Administrative Support Associate
Administrative Technician
Administrator
Certified Administrative Professional (CAP)
Certified Legal Secretary Specialist (CLSS)
Certified Manager (CM)
Certified Professional Secretary (CPS)
Clerk
Clerk Typist
Computer Operator
Corporate Administrative Officer (CAO)
Corporate Secretary
Department Secretary
Departmental Administrator
Desktop Publisher
Director of Administration
Director of Administrative Operations
Division Secretary

Administration, Office Management & Secretarial Services

Executive Administrative Assistant
Executive Administrative Associate
Executive Assistant
Executive Secretary
Front Office Manager
Legal Secretary
Mail Clerk
Mail Distribution Manager
Mail Superintendent
Manager of Administrative Services
Medical Office Manager
Medical Records Manager
Medical Secretary
Office Administrator
Office Assistant
Office Clerk
Office Coordinator
Office Manager
Office Services Manager
Office Support Services Manager
Patient Records Manager
Postmaster
Professional Legal Secretary (PLS)
Receptionist
Secretary
Stenographer
Support Services Manager
Telecommunications Operator
Telephone Operator
Transcriptionist
Typesetter
Typist
Vice President of Administration
Word Processor

Software, Systems & Technology

Administrative Software
Adobe Acrobat
Adobe Illustrator
Adobe Pagemaker
Corel WordPerfect
Data Entry Software
Database Query Software
Database Software
dBase Plus
FileMaker Pro
Graphic Design Software
Graphics Software
Hypertext Markup Language (HTML)
IBM Lotus 1-2-3
IBM Lotus Notes
ICVerify
IDX Groupcast
Intuit QuickBooks
Legal Terminology Software
Macromedia Dreamweaver
Medical Terminology Software
Microsoft Access
Microsoft Excel
Microsoft Outlook
Microsoft PowerPoint
Microsoft Project
Microsoft Windows
Microsoft Word
Presentation Software
Scientific Terminology Software
Spreadsheet Software
Technical Terminology Software

KeyWords & KeyWord Phrases for Administration, Office Management & Secretarial Services

Account Relations
Account Retention
Account Service
Administration
Administrative Infrastructure
Administrative Management
Administrative Office Management
Administrative Policies
Administrative Procedures
Administrative Processes
Administrative Services
Administrative Support
Administrative Support Services
Appointment Scheduling
Back Office Operations
Billing
Board Meeting Agenda
Board Meetings
Board of Directors
Budget
Budget Administration
Budget Management
Budgeting
Business Law
Business Mathematics
Business Principles
Cash
Cash Management
Cash Reconciliation
Clerical
Clerical Staff
Client Communications
Client Relations
Client Relationship Management

Client Satisfaction
Client Services
Clients
Committee
Committee Agenda
Committee Meeting
Communications
Composition
Conference
Conference Call
Conference Management
Conference Planning
Conference Scheduling
Confidential Correspondence
Confidential Correspondence Management
Confidential Correspondence Preparation
Contract Administration
Contracts
Copier
Corporate Document
Corporate Recordkeeping
Corporate Records
Corporate Report
Correspondence
Correspondence Management
Correspondence Preparation
Customer Complaint
Customer Complaint Resolution
Customer Inquiry
Customer Relations
Customer Relationship Management (CRM)
Customer Retention
Customer Satisfaction
Customer Service
Customers
Data Analysis
Data Collection
Data Entry
Database Administration

Administration, Office Management & Secretarial Services

Database Management
Desktop Publishing
Dictation
Digital Data
Digital Graphics
Digital Images
Document
Document Management
Editing
Efficiency Improvement
Electronic Communication
Electronic File
Electronic Information
Electronic Media
Electronic Page Layout
Electronic Publishing
Electronic Recordkeeping
Email
English
English Composition
English Grammar
English Language
Equipment Leasing
Executive Liaison
Executive Liaison Affairs
Executive Officer Support
Expense Control
Expense Documentation
Expense Reporting
Expenses
Facilities Management
Fax
Fax Machine
Files
Files Management
Filing
Financial Statement
Financial Statement Preparation
Forms

Forms Design
Forms Management
Front Office Operations
General Accounting
Government Affairs
Government Regulations
Government Reporting
Grammar
Graphic Design
Graphics
Incoming Correspondence
Incoming Correspondence Distribution
Incoming Correspondence Management
Incoming Correspondence Sorting
Information
Information Dissemination
Information Management
Information Requests
Information Storage Systems
Institute of Certified Professional Managers (ICPM)
Institute of Office Management & Administration (IOMA)
International Association of Administrative Professionals (IAAP)
Internet Research
Interpersonal Relations
Inventory Control
Inventory Management
Inventory Planning
Invoice
Invoice Preparation
Keyboarding
Leasing
Legal Secretarial Services
Letter
Letter Preparation
Liaison Affairs
Library Services
Logistics
Mail & Messenger Services
Mail Distribution

Administration, Office Management & Secretarial Services

Mail Distribution Management
Mail Distribution Operations
Mail Services
Mailroom
Management Principles
Materials
Materials Management
Mathematics
Medical Secretarial Services
Meeting
Meeting Agenda
Meeting Management
Meeting Planning
Meeting Scheduling
Memo
Memo Preparation
Memoranda
Memoranda Preparation
Memorandum
Memorandum Preparation
Messenger Services
Multi-Line Phone System
Office
Office Automation
Office Equipment
Office Equipment Budget
Office Files
Office Management
Office Materials
Office Procedures
Office Records
Office Security
Office Services
Office Supplies
Office Supplies Management
Office Supplies Ordering
Office Supplies Recordkeeping
Office Supplies Reordering
Office Support

Office Support Services
Office Support Services Management
Office Technology
Office Terminology
Oral Communications
Organization
Page Design
Page Layout
Paper Files
Phone System
Photographic Reproduction
Policies & Procedures
Printing
Private Branch Exchange (PBX)
Product Support
Productivity Improvement
Professional Services
Project Administration
Project Management
Project Scheduling
Property Management
Publishing
Punctuation
Purchasing
Reception Services
Recordkeeping
Records
Records Management
Records Management Systems
Regulations
Regulatory Compliance
Regulatory Reporting
Report Preparation
Reporting
Reports
Reproduction
Resource Allocation
Resource Management
Scheduling

Administration, Office Management & Secretarial Services

Secretarial Services
Security
Service Standards
Shipping
Spelling
Spreadsheet
Statistical Reporting
Statistics
Stenography
Storage
Supplies
Supply Inventory
Supply Management
Supply Ordering
Supply Recordkeeping
Supply Reporting
Support Services
Support Services Management
Team Building
Team Leadership
Technical Documentation
Technical Support
Technology Management
Telecommunications
Telecommunications Management
Temporary Staffing
Text Management
Time Management
Training & Development
Transcription
Transportation
Travel
Travel Arrangements
Travel Management
Travel Planning
Typeset
Typesetting
Typography
VIP Relations

Visitor Management
Visitor Reception
Visual Graphics
Warehousing
Word Processing
Workflow Planning & Prioritization
Workload Planning & Prioritization
Writing
Written Communications

Administration, Office Management & Secretarial Services

Legal Secretarial Services

Refer to Law Chapter for a detailed listing of law and legal keywords and keyword phrases.

Administrative Law
Affidavit
Agreement
Appeal
Business Law
Case
Case File
Case Law
Civil Law
Civil Litigation
Client Deposition
Client Hearing
Client Interview
Complaints
Constitutional Law
Copyright Law
Corporate Law
Corporate Minutes
Corporate Recordkeeping
Court
Court Decision
Court Official
Court Proceedings
Court Trial
Courtroom
Courtroom Official
Courtroom Proceedings
Courtroom Trial
Criminal Law
Criminal Record
Deposition
Elder Law
Employment Law
Employment Record
Estate Law

Family Law
Health Care Law
Hearing
Insurance Law
Intellectual Property
International Law
Labor Law
Law
Law Library
Legal Affairs
Legal Agreement
Legal Case
Legal Case File
Legal Correspondence
Legal Document
Legal Document Preparation
Legal Document Recording
Legal Document Reporting
Legal Papers
Legal Procedures
Legal Research
Legal Secretaries International (LSI)
Legal Terminology
Legal Writing
Medical Records
Motion
National Association of Legal Secretaries (NALS)
Patent Law
Personal Injury Law
Pretrial Agreement
Probate Law
Property Law
Real Estate Law
Subpoena
Summons
Tax Law
Tort
Transactions Law
Trial

Administration, Office Management & Secretarial Services

Trial Administration
Trial Preparation
Witness
Workers' Compensation

Finding Needles in a Haystack

Medical Secretarial Services

Refer to Health Care, Dental and Pharmacy Chapters for detailed listinsg of medical, pharmaceutical, dental and health care keywords and keyword phrases for all health care disciplines and specializations.

Appointment
Appointment Scheduling
Billing
Collections
Diagnostic Appointment
Doctor Relations
Doctors
Front Office
Front Office Management
Insurance
Insurance Authorization
Insurance Billing
Insurance Pre-Authorization
Insurance Reimbursement
Laboratory (Lab)
Laboratory (Lab) Results
Laboratory (Lab) Results Filing
Laboratory (Lab) Results Recordkeeping
Laboratory (Lab) Results Reporting
Legal Medical Terminology
Medical
Medical Charts
Medical Correspondence
Medical Histories
Medical Law
Medical Office
Medical Office Management
Medical Records
Medical Records Filing
Medical Records Management
Medical Reports
Medical Specialist

Administration, Office Management & Secretarial Services

Medical Terminology
Patient Billing
Patient Charts
Patient Correspondence
Patient Interviews
Patient Medical Histories
Patient Records
Patient Records Filing
Patient Records Management
Patient Relations
Patient Retention
Patient Satisfaction
Patient Services
Patients
Physician Relations
Physicians
Records
Records Filing
Records Management
Specialist
Surgery
Surgical Appointment

Add Your Own Keywords & Keyword Phrases

Chapter 3

Advertising & Corporate Communications

Principal Keyword List:

Advertising & Corporate Communications

Additional Keyword Lists:

Legal Secretarial Services
Medical Secretarial Services

Representative Job Titles

Account Executive
Account Manager
Advertising Campaign Manager
Advertising Director
Advertising Manager
Advertising Promotions Manager
Advertising Scriptwriter
Advertising Spokesperson
Art Director
Billboard Advertising Designer
Billboard Advertising Manager
Brand Manager
Broadcast Advertising Designer
Broadcasting Advertising Manager
Brochure Designer
Cable Advertising Designer
Cable Advertising Manager
Campaign Director
Campaign Manager
Classified Advertising Designer
Classified Advertising Manager
Communications Director
Communications Manager
Copy Writer
Corporate Communications Director
Corporate Communications Manager
Corporate Communications Specialist
Corporate Logo Designer
Creative Designer
Creative Director
Desktop Publisher
Desktop Publisher
Directory Advertising Designer
Directory Advertising Manager
Display Advertising Director
Display Advertising Manager

Advertising & Corporate Communications

Editor
Electronic Publishing Specialist
Film Editor
Fine Artist
Graphic Artist
Graphic Arts
Graphic Communications
Graphic Designer
Graphic Designer
Illustrator
Internet Advertising Designer
Internet Advertising Manager
Internet Copy Writer
Internet Designer
Internet Page Designer
Internet Page Layout Artist
Layout Artist
Layout Artist
Logo Designer
Magazine Advertising Designer
Magazine Advertising Manager
Media Advertising Designer
Media Advertising Manager
Media Buyer
Media Manager
Mock-Up Designer
Newspaper Advertising Designer
Newspaper Advertising Manager
Online Advertising Designer
Online Advertising Manager
Outdoor Advertising Designer
Outdoor Advertising Manager
Page Layout Artist
Periodicals Advertising Designer
Periodicals Advertising Manager
Photography Layout Designer
Point-of-Sale (POS) Advertising Designer
Point-of-Sale (POS) Advertising Manager
Point-of-Sale (POS) Promotions Designer

Point-of-Sale (POS) Promotions Manager
Print Advertising Designer
Print Advertising Manager
Print Layout Artist
Print Media Buyer
Project Manager
Project Planner
Promotional Advertising Designer
Promotional Advertising Manager
Promotions Designer
Promotions Director
Promotions Manager
Radio Advertising Designer
Radio Advertising Manager
Retail Advertising Designer
Retail Advertising Manager
Scriptwriter
Television Advertising Designer
Television Advertising Manager
Typographer
Vice President of Advertising
Vice President of Corporate Communications
Video Editor
Video Production Manager
Visual Artist
Web Publications Designer
Website Advertising Designer
Website Advertising Manager
Website Designer
Website Graphic Artist

Advertising & Corporate Communications

Software, Systems & Technology

Adobe Acrobat
Adobe Illustrator
Adobe Pagemaker
Adobe Photoshop
Atlas OnePoint
Corel WordPerfect
FileMaker Pro
Graphic Presentation Software
Graphics Software
IBM Lotus 1-2-3
IBM Lotus Notes
Intuit QuickBooks
Macromedia Dreamweaver
Macromedia Fireworks
Macromedia Flash
Macromedia Freehand
Media Professional
Mediamix
Microsoft Access
Microsoft Excel
Microsoft Office
Microsoft Outlook
Microsoft PowerPoint
Microsoft Project
Microsoft Windows
Microsoft Word
Project Management Software
Rain Catcher Inspire
Spreadsheet Software
Unisys Advertising Manager
Web Page Creation Software
Web Page Editing Software

Keywords & Keywords Phrases for Advertising & Corporate Communications

Search Tip:
You can use the words "advertising," "advertisement," and "ad" interchangeably, and the words "copy writer" and "copywriter" interchangeably.

Account
Account Billing
Account Management
Account Servicing
Ad
Advertisement
Advertising
Advertising Agency
Advertising Brochure
Advertising Budget
Advertising Budget Development
Advertising Budget Management
Advertising Campaign
Advertising Campaign Development
Advertising Campaign Management
Advertising Campaign Plan
Advertising Communications
Advertising Contract
Advertising Contract Management
Advertising Copy
Advertising Design
Advertising Development
Advertising Display
Advertising Layout
Advertising Management
Advertising Planning
Advertising Promotions
Advertising Script
Advertising Script Writing
Advertising Space
Advertising Strategy
American Advertising Federation (AAF)

Advertising & Corporate Communications

American Association of Advertising Agencies (AAAA)
Animation
Annual Reports
Art
Artwork
Banner Advertisements
Banners
Billboard
Billboard Advertising
Billboard Advertising Campaign
Billboard Advertising Design
Brand
Brand Concept
Brand Identity
Brand Integrity
Brand Management
Branding
Broadcast
Broadcast Advertising
Broadcast Advertising Campaign
Broadcast Advertising Design
Broadcast Advertising Management
Brochure
Brochure Design
Brochure Layout
Business Card Design
Business Cards
Buyer Targets
Buyers
Cable Advertising
Cable Advertising Campaign
Cable Advertising Design
Cable Advertising Management
Cable Advertising Manager
Campaign
Campaign Design
Campaign Development
Campaign Management
Campaign Manager

Campaign Plan
Campaign Plan Development
Campaign Plan Management
Catalog
Catalog Design
Catalog Designer
Classified Advertising
Classified Advertising Campaign
Classified Advertising Design
Classified Advertising Management
Click-Through Advertising
Collateral Materials
Collaterals
Color
Color Separation
Communications
Communications Management
Communications Media
Composition
Computer Graphics
Computer Software
Computer Technology
Computer-Aided Design & Drafting (CADD)
Computer-Aided Design (CAD)
Contests
Contract Management
Contracts
Copy
Copy Writing
Corporate Communications
Corporate Identity
Corporate Identity Campaign
Corporate Image
Corporate Image Campaign
Corporate Logo
Corporate Logo Design
Corporate Logo Development
Corporate Logo Placement
Corporate Mission

Advertising & Corporate Communications

Corporate Vision
Coupons
Creative
Creative Design
Creative Media
Creativity
Design
Desktop Publishing
Digital Data
Digital Graphics
Digital Images
Direct Mail
Direct Mail Advertising
Direct Mail Pieces
Direct Response
Direct Response Advertising
Direct Response Pieces
Directory Advertising
Directory Advertising Campaign
Directory Advertising Design
Directory Advertising Management
Directory Publishing
Display Advertising
Display Advertising Campaign
Display Advertising Design
Display Advertising Management
Editing
Editor
Electronic Advertising
Electronic Information
Electronic Media
Electronic Page Layout
Electronic Publishing
Film Editing
Film Production
Fine Arts
Graphic Arts
Graphic Communications
Graphic Design

Graphics
Icons
Illustration
Images
Incentives
Interactive Media
Internet Advertising
Internet Advertising Campaign
Internet Advertising Design
Internet Advertising Management
Internet Copy Writing
Internet Page Design
Internet Page Layout
Internet Publishing
Layout
Logo
Logo Design
Logo Development
Logo Placement
Magazine Advertising
Magazine Advertising Campaign
Magazine Advertising Design
Magazine Advertising Management
Magazines
Marketing Brochure
Marketing Communications
Media
Media Advertising
Media Advertising Campaign
Media Advertising Design
Media Advertising Management
Media Buying
Media Events
Media Management
Media Representative Firm
Media Sourcing
Messaging
Mock-Up Design
Multimedia

Advertising & Corporate Communications

Multimedia Advertising
Multimedia Technology
Newspaper Advertising
Newspaper Advertising Campaign
Newspaper Advertising Design
Newspaper Advertising Management
Newspaper Association of America (NAA)
Newspaper Inserts
Online Advertising
Online Advertising Campaign
Online Advertising Design
Online Advertising Management
Oral Media
Outdoor Advertising
Outdoor Advertising Campaign
Outdoor Advertising Design
Outdoor Advertising Management
Page Design
Page Layout
Periodicals
Periodicals Advertising
Periodicals Advertising Campaign
Periodicals Advertising Design
Periodicals Advertising Management
Photographic Reproduction
Photography
Photography Layout
Photography Layout Design
Point-of-Sale (POS) Advertising
Point-of-Sale (POS) Advertising Campaign
Point-of-Sale (POS) Advertising Design
Point-of-Sale (POS) Advertising Management
Point-of-Sale (POS) Promotions
Point-of-Sale (POS) Promotions Design
Point-of-Sale (POS) Promotions Management
Posters
Press Releases
Print
Print Advertising

Print Advertising Campaign
Print Advertising Design
Print Advertising Management
Print Layout
Print Media
Print Production
Print Publishing
Printing
Product Advertising
Product Advertising Campaign
Product Advertising Design
Product Advertising Management
Product Brochure
Product Literature
Project
Project Management
Project Planning
Project Scheduling
Project Staffing
Promotional Advertising
Promotional Advertising Campaign
Promotional Advertising Design
Promotional Advertising Management
Promotional Display
Promotional Events
Promotional Incentives
Promotions
Promotions Design
Promotions Management
Public Relations
Publicity
Radio Advertising
Radio Advertising Campaign
Radio Advertising Design
Radio Advertising Management
Radio Promotions
Radio Spot
Retail Advertising
Retail Advertising Campaign

Advertising & Corporate Communications

Retail Advertising Management
Retail Display Advertising
Retail Display Advertising Campaign
Script
Scripting
Scriptwriting
Service Advertising
Sign
Signage
Special Events
Sweepstakes
Technical Illustrations
Television
Television Advertising
Television Advertising Campaign
Television Advertising Design
Television Advertising Management
Television Promotions
Television Spot
Typeset
Typography
Video
Video Editing
Video Production
Video Production Management
Visual Arts
Visual Communications
Visual Elements
Visual Media
Website Advertising
Website Advertising Campaign
Website Advertising Design
Website Advertising Management
Website Design
Website Graphics
Written Media

Add Your Own Keywords & Keyword Phrases

Chapter 4

Architecture

Principal Keyword List:

Architecture

Additional Keyword Lists:

Drafting
Landscape Architecture
Surveying

Representative Job Titles

Architect
Architectural Drafter
Architectural Draftsman
Architectural Draftsperson
Architectural Engineer
Building Engineer
Civil Drafter
Computer-Aided Design & Drafting (CADD) Operator
Computer-Aided Design & Drafting (CADD) Technician
Computer-Aided Design (CAD) Operator
Computer-Aided Design (CAD) Technician
Design Architect
Design Engineer
Designer
Drafter
Draftsman
Draftsperson
Environmental Design
Environmental Planner
Field Crew Chief
Garden Designer
Golf Course Architect
Golf Course Designer
Instrument Man (I-Man)
Land Planner
Land Surveyor
Landscape Architect
Landscape Designer
Licensed Land Surveyor
Mechanical Drafter
Mine Surveyor
Model Maker
Professional Engineer
Professional Land Surveyor
Project Architect
Project Director

Architecture

Project Manager
Project Manager
Property Surveyor
Rodman
Space Design Architect
Space Designer
Spatial Design Architect
Spatial Designer
Structural Designer
Survey Crew Chief
Survey Party Chief
Survey Technician
Surveying Technician
Surveyor
Vice President of Architectural Engineering
Vice President of Architecture

Software, Systems & Technology

1CadCam Unigraphics
3-D Modeling Software
3-D Motion Capture Software
3-D Scanning Software
3-D Solid Modeling Software
Adobe Acrobat
Adobe Illustrator
Adobe LiveMotion
Adobe Photoshop
ArchiOffice Software
ARCOM Masterspec
ARCOM Masterspec
Autodesk Architectural Desktop
Autodesk AutoCAD
Autodesk AutoCAD Blue Sky
Autodesk AutoCAD Mechanical
Cadence Allegro Design Entry Software
CADFind Sketch & Search Software
CD-adapco STAR-CAD
CMT Incorporate CogoCAD
Computer-Aided Design & Drafting (CADD) Software
Computer-Aided Design (CAD) Software
Computer-Based Training Software
Coordinate Geometry (COGO) Software
Corel WordPerfect
Cosmo Software Cosmo World
Cost Estimating Software
Craftsman CD Estimator
Database Software
Design Specification Database Software
Development Environment Software
Digital Elevation Model (DEM) Software
Digital Image Correlation (DIC) Software
Document Management Software
ESRI ArcEditor
ESRI ArcGIS

Architecture

ESRI ArcInfo
ESRI ArcView
ESRI ArcView 3D Analyst
Facilities Planning Software
FileMaker Pro
Geomechanical Design Analysis (GDA) Software
Graphic Presentation Software
Graphics Software
Hewlett Packard SolidDesigner
IBM Lotus 1-2-3
IBM Lotus Notes
Image Analysis System
Intergraph Image Analyst
Intergraph INtools
Intuit QuickBooks
JD Edwards EnterpriseOne Project Management
Kubotek CADkey
Logitech 3D Pro
Macromedia Dreamweaver
Macromedia Fireworks
Macromedia Flash
Macromedia Freehand
Map Creation Software
Materials Requirements Planning (MRP) Software
Mathsoft MathCAD
Mathworks MATLAB
Mentor Graphics ModelSlim
Micro-Press MicroStation PowerDraft
Microsoft Access
Microsoft Excel
Microsoft Outlook
Microsoft PowerPoint
Microsoft Project
Microsoft Visio
Microsoft Visual Basic
Microsoft Visual Studio
Microsoft Windows
Microsoft Word
MicroSurvey FieldGenius

MicroSurvey Software
OrCAD Capture
PC Mapper Software
PCI Geomatics Software
Photo-Imaging Software
Physical Design Software
Presentation Software
Pro-E CAD
Project Analysis & Costing Software
Project Management Software
PTC Pro/ENGINEER
PTC Pro/INTRALINK
PTC Pro/MECHANICAL
Rand McNally World Digital Database
Realization Project Flow
Relational Database Software
Requirements Management Software
Road Design Software
Roof Builder Tools Software
Roof Support Design Software
Root Cause Analysis Software
Safety, Health & Environmental Management Software
Scanning Software
Scientific Software
SketchUp Software
SKILL
SofTech CADRA
Softimage Extreme
SoftLab PHEdesign
SiteComp Software
Sokkia G2
Sokkia Imap
Sokkia Spectrum Survey Suite
SolidWorks CAD
Spreadsheet Software
Statistical Analysis Software
Statistical Energy Analysis (SEA) Software
Surface Modeling Software
Survey Software

Architecture

Survey Starnet Software
Thermal Analysis Systems The Energy Analyst
Thermal Indoor Climate Simulation Software
Trimble Digital Fieldbook
Trimble GPS Pathfinder
Trimble TerraSync
Tripod Data Systems Foresight
Tripod Data Systems COGO
Virtual Reality Modeling Language (VRML) Software
Zone Modeling Software

KeyWords & KeyWord Phrases for Architecture, Drafting, Landscape Architecture & Surveying

Aesthetic Design
Algebra
American Design Drafting Association (ADDA)
American Institute of Architects (AIA)
Architect
Architect's Scale
Architectural Concept
Architectural Corrections
Architectural Designs
Architectural Drafting
Architectural Drawings
Architectural Elements
Architectural Engineering
Architectural Plans
Architectural Renderings
Architectural Specifications
Architecture
Arithmetic
Arm Drafting Machine
Athletic Center
Athletic Complex
Athletic Facility
Blueprints
Budget
Budget Administration
Budgeting
Building
Building By-Laws
Building Codes
Building Contract
Building Contract Documents
Building Plans
Building Site
Building Site Requirements

Architecture

Building Site Restrictions
Calculus
Capital Project
Charts
Client Negotiations
Client Presentations
Client Relations
Client Requirements
College
College Building
College Complex
College Facility
Color
Color Specification
Commercial
Commercial Building
Commercial Building Design
Commercial Design
Computer Analysis
Computer Applications
Computer Programming
Computer Simulation
Computer Software
Computer Systems
Computer-Aided Design & Drafting (CADD)
Computer-Aided Design (CAD)
Computer-Aided Engineering (CAE)
Concept
Conceptual Design
Configuration
Construction
Construction Project
Construction Project Management
Conventional Drafting
Conventional Drafting Station
Cost
Cost Analysis
Cost Budget
Cost Effectiveness

Cost Estimate
Customer Management
Customer Relations
Customer Requirements
Data Acquisition
Data Analysis
Data Capture
Data Collection
Data Interpretation
Data Reporting
Design
Design Architecture
Design Concept
Design Corrections
Design Elements
Design Layout
Design Modification
Design Parameters
Design Plans
Design Principles
Design Requirements
Design Specifications
Design Techniques
Design Tools
Digitizer
Dimensions
Dimensions Configuration
Documentation
Drafting
Drafting Equipment
Drafting Equipment Calibration
Drafting Tools
Drainage
Drawings
Educational Building
Educational Complex
Educational Facility
Electrical Design
Electrical Systems Design

Architecture

Electronics
Electronics Equipment
Engineering Bulletins
Engineering Calculations
Engineering Change Order (ECO)
Engineering Data
Engineering Data Analysis
Engineering Documentation
Engineering Drawings
Engineering Mathematics
Engineering Modification
Engineering Plans
Engineering Principles
Engineering Schematics
Engineering Science
Engineering Specifications
Engineering Techniques
Engineering Technology
Ergonomic Techniques
Expense Control
Experimental Design
Fabricate
Fabrication
Fabrication Parameters
Facilities
Facilities Design
Factory
Feasibility
Feasibility Analysis
Final Customer Acceptance
Foundation
Geographic Information System (GIS)
Geographic Positioning System (GPS)
Geomechanical Design Analysis (GDA)
Government Buildings
Graphs
Health Care Clinic
Health Care Facility
Hospital

Industrial Complex
Industrial Plant
Inspection
Inspection Report
Layout Drawings
Manufacturing Complex
Manufacturing Plant
Master Sketches
Material Dynamics
Materials
Materials Specification
Mathematical Modeling
Mathematical Models
Mathematics
Measurement
Measurement Equipment
Measurement Instrumentation
Measurement Instruments
Mechanical Design
Mechanical Systems Design
Model
Model Making
Modification
National Council of Architectural Registration Boards (NCARB)
National Society of Architectural Engineers (NSAE)
Office
Office Building
Office Complex
Physical Applications
Physical Laws
Physical Principles
Physics
Prison
Project
Project Architecture
Project Budget
Project Budget Administration
Project Budgeting
Project Contract

Architecture

Project Contract Administration
Project Cost
Project Cost Estimate
Project Feasibility
Project Layout
Project Management
Project Planning
Project Specifications
Project Work-Time Estimate
Quality
Recreational Center
Recreational Complex
Recreational Facility
Regulations
Regulatory Affairs
Regulatory Compliance
Regulatory Reporting
Residential
Residential Building Design
Residential Design
Resources
Safety
Safety Regulations
Safety Standards
Scale Drawings
Scale Plans
Schematics
School
School Building
Site
Site Requirements
Site Restrictions
Sketch
Sketches
Space
Space Design
Space Layout
Space Management
Space Optimization

Space Planning
Space Requirements
Space Utilization
Spatial
Spatial Design
Spatial Layout
Spatial Management
Spatial Planning
Spatial Requirements
Specification Documents
Specification Sheets
Specifications
Sporting Center
Sporting Complex
Sporting Facility
Sports Center
Sports Complex
Sports Facility
Statistical Analysis
Statistics
Strength
Strength Evaluation System
Structural Design
Structural Planning
Structure Specifications
Structures
Tables
Technical Briefings
Technical Documentation
Technical Drawings
Technical Handbooks
Technical Instructions
Technical Plans
Technical Reports
Technical Writing
Theoretical Model
Track Drafting
Track Drafting Machine
Unified Design

Architecture

University
University Building
University Complex
University Facility
Wiring Diagrams
Working Drawings
Working Model
Work-Time Estimate

Additional Keywords & Keywords Phrases for Landscape Architecture

American Society of Landscape Architects (ASLA)
Council of Landscape Architectural Registraion Boards
Decorative Features
Decorative Garden
Decorative Landscaping
Environmental
Environmental Design
Environmental Impact
Environmental Impact Analysis
Flowering Plants
Flowering Trees
Flowers
Fountains
Garden
Garden Architecture
Garden Design
Geological Analysis
Geological Survey
Geology
Golf Course Architecture
Golf Course Design
Land Development
Land Features
Land Planning
Land Preparation
Land Structures
Landscape Architect Registration Examination (LARE)
Landscape Architecture
Landscape Design
Landscape Ecology
Landscaping
Landscaping Plans
Natural Resource Management
Natural Resource Conservation
Natural Resource Preservation

Architecture

Parks
Paths
Plant Rotation
Plant Science
Planting
Plants
Playgrounds
Public Gardens
Public Lands
Public Parks
Recreational Parks
Rock Gardens
Rocks
Seedlings
Shrubs
Soil Science
Stones
Storm Water Management
Storm Water Run-Off
Street & Highway Beautification
Topography
Traffic Design
Traffic Management
Trees
Vegetation
Walkways
Water
Water Cascades
Water Fountains
Water Science
Waterfront Improvement
Wetlands Preservation
Wetlands Restoration

Additional Keywords & Keywords Phrases for Surveying

3-D Laser Scanning System
American Association of Geodetic Surveying (AAGS)
American Congress on Surveying & Mapping (ACSM)
Angle
The Imaging & Geospatial Information Society (ASPRS)
Atmospheric Impact
Atmospheric Impact Analysis
Automatic Level
Automatic Optical Pendulum Leveling System
Azimuth
Baseline
Boundary
Boundary Surveys
Cartography
Compass
Construction
Contour
Coordinates
Cross Section
Cross-Section Elevation
Deed
Depth
Descriptive Data
Dimension
Direct Elevation Road
Distance
Distance Meter
Dot Laser
Earth Curvature
Earth Curvature Corrections
Echosounder
Electronic Digital Level
Electronic Digital Theodolite
Electronic Distance-Measuring Device
Electronic Distance-Measuring Equipment
Electrotape

Architecture

Elevation
Fathometer
Field Crew
Gammon Reel
Geodesics
Geodetic Measurements
Geomechanical
Geomechanical Design
Geospatial
Gravitation
Ground
Ground Survey
Hand Level
Height
Inked Tracings
Instrument Operations
Instrument Maintenance
Instrument Repair
Invisible Beam Laser
Land
Land Boundary
Land Boundary Surveys
Land Contour
Land Deed
Land Dimension
Land Elevation
Land Evaluation
Land Features
Land Gravitation
Land Legal Description
Land Location
Land Shape
Land Survey
Land Surveying
Land Title
Laser
Laser Distance-Measuring Equipment
Laser Equipment
Laser Level

Laser Measuring System
Laser Scanner Coordinate Capturing Equipment
Laser Technology
Legal Description
Legal Deed
Legal Title
Level
Level Runs
Leveling Bubbles
Location
Long-Range Reflectorless Total Station
Man-Made Structures
Map
Mapmaking
Mapping
Marker Placement
Markers
Measurements
Measuring Chain
Measuring Rod
Mine Survey
Mining
Multibeam Sonar Equipment
Muncy Plat Pronto
National Council of Examiners for Engineering & Surveying (NCEES)
National Society of Professional Surveyors (NSPS)
Natural Features
Optical Pendulum Level
Philadelphia Rod
Plat
Plot
Plotting
Precision Level
Prism
Property Boundary
Property Boundary Surveys
Property Contour
Property Deed
Property Dimension

Architecture

Property Elevation
Property Evaluation
Property Features
Property Gravitation
Property Irons
Property Legal Description
Property Lines
Property Location
Property Shape
Property Survey
Property Surveying
Property Title
Robotic Total Station
Rotary Laser
San Francisco Rod
Section Corners
Shape
Side-Scan Sonar
Sighting
Sonar
Surface
Survey
Survey Crew
Survey Data
Survey Data Analysis
Survey Data Collection
Survey Data Extrapolation
Survey Data Interpretation
Survey Data Reporting
Survey Instruments
Survey Measurements
Survey Points
Survey Records
Survey Sites
Surveying
Surveying Equipment
Surveying Equipment Calibration
Surveying Equipment Management
Surveying Instruments

Surveyor's Leveling Rod
Tellurometer
Theodolite
Theodolite Distance-Measuring Equipment
Theodolite Operator
Title
Total Field Station
Total Station
Traverse
Traverse Adjustment
Traverse Closure
Tribrach Level Bubble Adjusting Block
Tribrach Optical Plummet Adjusting Cylinder
Underground
Underwater
Vertical Rods
Visible Beam Laser

Architecture

Add Your Own Keywords & Keyword Phrases

Chapter 5

Art & Design

Principal Keyword Lists:

Commercial & Industrial Design
Graphic Arts, Graphic Design & Art Direction
Interior Design

Representative Job Titles

3-D Designer
Acoustics Design Engineer
Acoustics Designer
Advertising Director
Advertising Manager
Animator
Art Director
Art Manager
Artist
Audio & Visual Equipment Technician
Bath Designer
Broadcast Technician
Catalog Designer
Certified Kitchen Designer (CKD)
Closet Designer
Color & Materials Designer
Commercial Designer
Commercial Interior Designer
Conceptual Designer
Copy Writer
Corporate Communications Director
Corporate Communications Manager
Corporate Communications Specialist
Creative Designer
Creative Director
Decorating Consultant
Design Engineer
Designer
Desktop Publisher
Director of Interiors
Editor
Electrical Designer
Electronic Page Layout Artist
Electronic Publishing Specialist
Environmental Graphics Designer
Ergonomic Designer

Art & Design

Film & Video Editor
Film Graphic Designer
Fine Artist
Furniture Designer
Graphic Artist
Graphic Arts Designer
Graphic Designer
Green Designer
Illustrator
Image Designer
Industrial Designer
Interior Decorator
Interior Design Consultant
Interior Design Coordinator
Internet Designer
Internet Page Designer
Internet Page Layout Artist
Kitchen Designer
Layout Artist
Logo Design Artist
Materials Designer
Materials Science
Mock-Up Designer
Mold Designer
Newspaper Designer
Newspaper Layout Artist
Package Designer
Packaging Designer
Page Designer
Page Layout Artist
Photographer
Photographic Designer
Print Designer
Product Designer
Product Development Engineer
Product Engineer
Production Manager
Project Manager
Project Planner

Prototype Designer
Space Designer
Space Planner
Strategic Designer
Technical Designer
Technical Graphic Designer
Typesetter
Typographer
Video Designer
Video Game Designer
Visual Artist
Visual Arts Designer
Visual Graphics Designer
Web Publications Designer
Website Designer
Work Space Designer
Writer

Art & Design

Software, Systems & Technology

1CadCam Unigraphics
3-D Modeling Software
3-D Solid Modeling Software
Adobe Acrobat
Adobe Illustrator
Adobe LiveMotion
Adobe Pagemaker
Adobe Photoshop
Atlas one point
Autodesk AutoCAD
Bill of Materials Software
Cadence Allegro Design Entry Software
Corel WordPerfect
Cost Estimating Software
Data Entry Software
Database Query Software
Database Software
Database User Interface Software
Design Specification Database Software
Digital Image Correlation (DIC) Software
Document Management Software
Electronic Design Automation (EDA) Software
Enterprise Resource Planning (ERP) Software
Facilities Planning Software
FileMaker Pro
Graphic Presentation Software
Graphics Software
Hewlett Packard SolidDesigner
IBM Lotus 1-2-3
IBM Lotus Notes
Intuit QuickBooks
JD Edwards EnterpriseOne Project Management
Kubotek CADkey
Logitech 3D Pro
Macromedia Dreamweaver
Macromedia Fireworks

Macromedia Flash
Macromedia Freehand
Materials Requirements Planning (MRP) Software
Media Professional
Mediamix
Microsoft Access
Microsoft Excel
Microsoft Office
Microsoft Outlook
Microsoft PowerPoint
Microsoft Project
Microsoft Windows
Microsoft Word
OrCAD Capture
Physical Design Software
Presentation Software
Pro-E CAD
Project Management Software
Quark
Requirements Management Software
Roof Support Design Software
SolidWorks CAD
Spreadsheet Software
Statistical Analysis Software
Thermal Indoor Climate Simulation Software
Virtual Reality Modeling Language (VRML) Software
Web Page Creation Software
Web Page Editing Software

Keywords & Keyword Phrases for Commercial & Industrial Design

3-D Design
3-D Images
Aesthetic Design
Aesthetic Quality
Airport Design
Appearance
Architectural Detailing
Architectural Review
Architecture
Artistic
Artwork
Automated Production Tools
Balance
Blueprints
Brand Identity
Brand Integrity
Branding
Building
Building Codes
Building Construction
Building Layout
Building Plans
Building Science
Building Security
Color
Commercial
Commercial Design
Commercial Property
Computer Graphics
Computer Software
Computer-Aided Design & Drafting (CADD)
Computer-Aided Design (CAD)
Computer-Aided Industrial Design (CAID)
Conceptual Design
Conceptual Diagram
Conceptual Sketches

Construction
Cost Estimates
Creative Design
Creativity
Design
Design Alteration
Design Alternative
Design Center
Design Committee
Design Concepts
Design Elements
Design Engineering
Design Feasibility
Design Programming
Design Tools
Design Trends
Diagram
Drafting
Drafting Instruments
Drawings
Energy
Energy Efficiency
Engineering
Environmental Design
Environmental Quality
Ergonomic Design
Ergonomics
Estimates
Estimation
Exhibitions
Feasibility
Feasibility Analysis
Function
Functional Design
Graphic Arts
Graphic Design
Graphics
Green Design
Health Care Facility

Art & Design

Hospital
Illustrations
Images
Industrial
Industrial Design
Industrial Designers Society of America (IDSA)
Industrial Engineering
Industrial Materials
Industrial Processes
Industrial Security
Interactive Media
Layout
Machine-Readable Instructions
Manufactured Goods
Manufacturing
Manufacturing Methods
Materials
Materials Science
Mathematics
Mock-Up Design
Modeling
Models
Mold Design
Multimedia
Multimedia Technology
National Association of Schools of Arts & Design (NASAD)
Noise Abatement
Ornamentation
Package Design
Packaging
Perspective
Photography
Physical Design
Physical Modeling
Physical Science
Product
Product Characteristics
Product Design
Product Development

Product Development Engineering
Product Engineering
Product Function
Product Look
Product Quality
Product Safety
Product Style
Production
Production Materials
Production Methods
Project
Project Management
Project Planning
Project Scheduling
Project Staffing
Proportion
Prototype
Prototype Development
Renderings
Safety
Safety Codes
Safety Testing
Samples
Security
Security Systems
Serviceability
Sign
Signage
Sketches
Space Planning
Spatial Planning
Specification Sheets
Specifications
Strategic Design
Strategic Vision
Style
Technical Design
Usability
Usability Testing

Art & Design

Video
Visual Elements
Work Space
Work Space Design
Working Drawings

Keywords & Keyword Phrases for Graphic Arts, Graphic Design & Art Direction

3-D Design
3-D Images
Ad
Advertising
Advertising Brochure
Advertising Campaign
Advertising Design
Advertising Layout
Advertising Space
American Institute of Graphic Arts
Animation
Art
Art Directors Club
Artwork
Book Publishing
Books
Brand Identity
Brand Integrity
Branding
Brochure
Catalog Design
Catalogs
Cellular Phones
Charts
Color
Color Separation
Communications
Composition
Computer Graphics
Computer Software
Computer-Aided Design & Drafting (CADD)
Computer-Aided Design (CAD)
Corporate Communications
Corporate Logo
Creative
Creative Design

Art & Design

Creativity
Design
Design Concepts
Design Elements
Design Solutions
Desktop Publishing
Digital Data
Digital Graphics
Digital Images
Directory Publishing
Drawings
Electronic Information
Electronic Media
Electronic Page Layout
Electronic Publishing
Environmental Graphics
Film Graphics
Film Media
Fine Arts
Graphic Arts
Graphic Arts Information Network (GAIN)
Graphic Communications
Graphic Communications Council (GCC)
Graphic Design
Graphics
Hypertext Markup Language (HTML)
Illustration
Images
Interactive Media
Internet Page Design
Internet Page Layout
Internet Publishing
Journal Publishing
Journals
Layout
Logo
Logo Design
Magazine Publishing
Magazines

Marketing Brochure
Marketing Communications (Marcomm)
Materials
Materials Selection
Materials Specification
Media
Messaging
Mock-Up Design
Models
Multimedia
Multimedia Technology
National Association of Schools of Arts & Design (NASAD)
Newspaper Design
Newspaper Layout
Newspapers
Package Design
Packaging
Page Design
Page Layout
Periodicals
Periodicals Publishing
Photographic Design
Photographic Reproduction
Photographs
Photography
Point-of-Sale (POS)
Point-of-Sale Design
Point-of-Sale Promotions
Presentation
Print Design
Print Layout
Print Media
Print Publishing
Printing
Product Brochure
Product Design
Product Literature
Product Packaging
Project

Art & Design

Project Management
Project Planning
Project Scheduling
Project Staffing
Promotional Advertising
Promotional Display
Promotions
Publications
Publishing
Sign
Signage
Sketches
Studio Art
Technical Design
Technical Graphic Design
Television Graphics
Type Size
Type Style
Typeset
Typography
Video
Video Design
Video Games
Video Graphics
Visual
Visual Arts
Visual Communications
Visual Design
Visual Elements
Visual Graphics
Visual Media
Website Design
Website Graphics

Keywords & Keyword Phrases for Interior Design

3-D Design
3-D Images
Accessories
Acoustics
Acoustics Design
ADA Compliance
Aesthetic Design
Aesthetic Quality
Aesthetics
Airport Design
American Disabilities Act (ADA)
American Society of Interior Designers (ASID)
Antiques
Architect
Architectural Detailing
Architectural Review
Architecture
Artistic
Artwork
Balance
Bath Design
Blueprints
Building
Building Codes
Building Construction
Building Layout
Building Plans
Building Science
Closet Design
Color
Color & Materials Design
Commercial
Commercial Interior Design
Commercial Property
Computer Graphics
Computer Software

Art & Design

Computer-Aided Design & Drafting (CADD)
Computer-Aided Design (CAD)
Conceptual Design
Conceptual Diagram
Conceptual Sketches
Construction
Creative Design
Creativity
Decor
Decorating
Design
Design Alterations
Design Alternatives
Design Center
Design Elements
Design Programming
Design Tools
Diagram
Doors
Drawings
Elder Design
Elevator
Energy
Energy Efficiency
Environmental Quality
Ergonomic Design
Ergonomics
Escalator
Fabrics
Fine Arts
Finishes
Fixtures
Floor Coverings
Foundation for Interior Design Education Research (FIDER)
Function
Functional Design
Furnishings
Furniture
Furniture Design

Green Design
Health Care Facilities
Historic
Historic Property
Historic Renovation
Historical
Home Improvement
Hospitals
Illustration
Images
Indoor Living Spaces
Interactive Media
Interior Decor
Interior Design
Interior Design Experience Program (IDEP)
Interior Space
Kitchen Design
Layout
Lighting
Materials
Materials Design
Materials Science
Mathematics
Mock-Up Design
Multimedia
Multimedia Technology
National Association of Schools of Art & Design (NASAD)
National Council Interior Design Qualifications (NCIDQ)
National Kitchen & Bath Association (NKBA)
New Construction
Noise Abatement
Offices
Outdoor Living Spaces
Perspective
Photography
Physical Design
Physical Modeling
Physical Science
Project Management

Art & Design

Project Planning
Project Scheduling
Project Staffing
Proportion
Recreational Property
Rehabilitation
Renderings
Renovation
Residential
Residential Property
Resort Property
Restaurants
Safety
Safety Codes
Samples
School
Security
Security Systems
Shopping Mall
Sketches
Space Design
Space Layout
Space Planning
Spatial Planning
Specifications
Stairway
Strategic Design
Strategic Vision
Style
Technical Design
Textures
Theater
Usability
Usability Testing
Visual Elements
Walkway
Window Coverings
Window Treatments
Windows

Add Your Own Keywords & Keyword Phrases

Chapter 6

Customer Service

Principal Keyword List:

Customer Service

Representative Job Titles

Account Administrator
Account Executive
Account Manager
Account Representative
Account Services Coordinator
Account Services Manager
Account Services Representative
Account Supervisor
Call Center Manager
Call Center Representative
Claims Service Manager
Claims Service Representative
Client Call Center Manager
Client Call Center Representative
Client Service Manager
Client Service Representative
Client Service Specialist
Client Services Manager
Client Services Vice President
Customer Acceptance Representative
Customer Account Manager
Customer Account Representative
Customer Call Center Manager
Customer Call Center Representative
Customer Loyalty Manager
Customer Relationship Manager
Customer Representative
Customer Service Associate
Customer Service Director
Customer Service Manager
Customer Service Representative (CSR)
Customer Service Specialist
Director of Account Relations
Director of Customer Service
Director of Sales Support
Key Account Representative

Customer Service

Key Account Service Manager
Key Account Service Representative
Major Account Representative
Major Account Service Representative
Member Services Manager
Member Services Representative
Sales Administrator
Sales Support Administrator
Sales Support Representative
Senior Vice President of Account Relations
Senior Vice President of Customer Service
Telephone Service Manager
Telephone Service Representative
Vice President of Account Relations
Vice President of Account Service
Vice President of Customer Service

Software, Systems & Technology

Active Data Online WebChat
Adobe Acrobat
Adobe Illustrator
Adobe Pagemaker
Astute Solutions PowerCenter
Atlas OnePoint GO TOAST
Austin Logistics CallSelect
Autodialing Systems
Avidian Technologies Prophet
Calling Line Identification Equipment
Click Tracks
Cognos 8 Business Intelligence
Corel WordPerfect
Databox
Dialed Number Identification Systems (DNIS)
Enterprise Resource Planning (ERP)
Epiphany
eStrate Softphone
Factiva
Fast Track Systems
FileMaker Pro
Focus
FrontRange Solutions Goldmine
Galilee Enterprise TargetPro
IBM DB2
IBM Lotus 1-2-3
IBM Lotus Notes
Informatica Corporation PowerCenter
Intellimed
Intuit QuickBooks
Key Survey
Khameleon Software E-Business Suite Special Edition
LexisNexis
Listserv
Mastermind
Microsoft Access

Customer Service

Microsoft Excel
Microsoft Outlook
Microsoft PowerPoint
Microsoft Project
Microsoft Windows
Microsoft Word
MicroStrategy Desktop
Multi-Channel Contact Center Software
Nedstate Sitestat
NetSuite NetCRM
Parature eRealTime
Perseus Survey Solutions
Predictive Dialer
SAP
SAP Business One
SAS
Soffront CRM Portal
Software on Sailboats Desktop Sales Manager
SSA Global
Structured Query Language (SQL)
Sybase iAnywhere Pharma Anyware
Sybase iAnywhere Sales Anywhere
Sybase Structured Query Language (SQL)
TechExcel
Telemation e-CRM
Tigerpaw
Timpani Chat
Timpani Contact Center
Timpani Email
Unistat Statistical Package
Vanguard Sales Manager
Vantage MCIF
WebEx Sales Center
WinCross

KeyWords & KeyWord Phrases for Customer Service

Account
Account Administration
Account Cancellation
Account Management
Account Relationship Management
Account Retention
Account Services
Administration
Benefits & Features
Bill Adjustments
Billing
Billing Arrangements
Brand
Brand Identity
Brand Integrity
Branding
Brochures
Budget
Budget Administration
Budget Development
Budget Management
Budgeting
Buyer
Buying Habits
Buying Trends
Call Center
Call Center Management
Catalogs
Category
Claims
Claims Investigation
Claims Service
Claims Service Management
Client Call Center
Client Call Center Management

Customer Service

Client Comments
Client Complaint Resolution
Client Complaints
Client Development
Client Focus Groups
Client Grievances
Client Inquiries
Client Interaction
Client Loyalty
Client Management
Client Needs Assessment
Client Presentations
Client Relationship Management (CRM)
Client Retention
Client Satisfaction
Client Service
Client Service Management
Client Services
Client Services Management
Client Surveys
Client Transactions
Communications
Communications Management
Computer Graphics
Computer Software
Computer Technology
Consumer Behavior
Consumer Brand
Consumer Buying Behavior
Consumer Packaged Goods
Contests
Corporate Brand
Corporate Identity
Corporate Image
Cross-Cultural Communications
Customer
Customer Account
Customer Billing
Customer Call Center

Customer Call Center Management
Customer Care
Customer Comments
Customer Communications
Customer Complaint Resolution
Customer Complaints
Customer Demographics
Customer Feedback
Customer Focus Groups
Customer Grievances
Customer Inquiries
Customer Interaction
Customer Loyalty
Customer Management
Customer Needs
Customer Needs Assessment
Customer Preferences
Customer Presentations
Customer Relationship Management (CRM)
Customer Retention
Customer Satisfaction
Customer Segmentation
Customer Service
Customer Service Management
Customer Survey
Customer Transactions
Data
Data Analysis
Data Collection
Direct Mail
Direct Mail Pieces
Direct Response Pieces
E-Business
E-Commerce
Electronic Commerce
Expense Control
Expense Reporting
Features & Benefits
Focus Group

Customer Service

Forecasting
Fulfillment
Global Markets
Graphic Design
Graphics
Headquarters Account Management
Inbound Service Operation
Incentive
Incentive Campaign
Inventory
Inventory Control
Inventory Management
Inventory Planning
Key Account Management
Key Account Relationship Management
Member Services
Member Services Management
Merchandise
Merchandise Exchange
Newsletters
Order Cancellations
Order Fulfillment
Order Processing
Orders
Outbound Service Operation
Payment Processing
Payment Recordkeeping
Payments
Policies & Procedures
Print Communications
Private Branding
Private Label
Process Simplification
Product Availability
Product Benefits
Product Catalog
Product Exchange
Product Features
Product Information

Product Launch
Product Literature
Product Management
Product Merchandising
Product Presentations
Product Promotions
Product Sales
Product Samples
Product Specifications
Profit & Loss (P&L)
Profit & Loss (P&L) Management
Profit Growth
Profitability Analysis
Project
Project Administration
Project Management
Promotions
Rebate
Recordkeeping
Records Management
Refunds
Relationship Management
Reporting
Retail
Sales
Sales Administration
Sales Incentive
Sales Orders
Service
Service Benchmark
Service Delivery
Service Information
Service Measures
Service Quality
Service Sales
Statistical Analysis
Statistics
Strategic Relationship Management
Survey

Customer Service

Sweepstakes
Team Building
Team Leadership
Technical Illustrations
Telemarketing
Telemarketing Operations
Telephone Service Management
Telesales
Telesales Operations
Training & Development
Transaction Processing
Virtual Administration
Website
Wholesale
Wholesale Account
Wholesale Account Service
Wholesale Account Service Management

Add Your Own Keywords & Keyword Phrases

Chapter 7

Equipment Installation, Maintenance & Repair

Many of the keyword lists in this chapter are for similar professions that you'll also find in the Engineering Chapter. As such, use the listings in both chapters for all of your keyword searches.

Principal Keyword List:

Installation, Maintenance & Repair - Equipment, Machinery, Technology & Vehicles

Additional Keyword Lists:

Aircraft & Avionics Equipment
Coin, Vending & Amusement Machines
Computer, ATM & Office Machines
Electrical & Electronic Systems, Equipment & Machines
Farm Equipment & Machinery
Heating, Ventilating, Air Conditioning & Refrigeration Systems
Industrial Equipment & Machinery
Medical Equipment & Technology
Radio & Telecommunications Equipment
Rigging
Vehicular Systems - Automotive, Motorboat, Motorcycle, Heavy Equipment, Small Engine & Diesel

Representative Job Titles

Agricultural Mechanic
Agricultural Technician
Air Conditioning Mechanic
Air Conditioning Systems Mechanic
Air Conditioning Systems Specialist
Air Conditioning Systems Technician
Air Conditioning Technician
Aircraft Electrical Systems Installer
Aircraft Electrical Systems Maintenance Technician
Aircraft Electrical Systems Mechanic
Aircraft Electrical Systems Service Technician
Aircraft Electrical Systems Specialist
Aircraft Electrical Systems Technician
Aircraft Maintenance Director
Aircraft Maintenance Mechanic
Aircraft Maintenance Service Technician
Aircraft Maintenance Supervisor
Aircraft Maintenance Technician
Aircraft Mechanic
Aircraft Restorer
Aircraft Service Mechanic
Aircraft Service Technician
Aircraft Technician
Airframe Maintenance Technician
Airframe Mechanic
Airframe Service Technician
Airframe Technician
Alignment Specialist
All Terrain Vehicle (ATV) Maintenance Mechanic
All Terrain Vehicle (ATV) Maintenance Technician
All Terrain Vehicle ATV) Technician
Amusement Equipment Installer
Amusement Equipment Maintenance Mechanic
Amusement Equipment Maintenance Technician
Amusement Equipment Service Technician
Amusement Equipment Technician

Equipment Installation, Maintenance & Repair

Amusement Machine Installer
Amusement Machine Maintenance Technician
Amusement Machine Service Technician
Amusement Machine Technician
Apprentice
Automated Teller Machine (ATM) Installer
Automated Teller Machine (ATM) Maintenance Mechanic
Automated Teller Machine (ATM) Maintenance Technician
Automated Teller Machine (ATM) Service Technician
Automated Teller Machine (ATM) Technician
Automotive Maintenance Mechanic
Automotive Maintenance Technician
Automotive Master Mechanic
Automotive Mechanic
Automotive Service Excellence (ASE) Master Mechanic
Automotive Service Technician
Automotive Specialty Technician
Automotive Technician
Aviation Electrical Technician
Aviation Maintenance Supervisor
Aviation Maintenance Technician
Aviation Mechanic
Aviation Systems Installer
Aviation Systems Maintenance Technician
Aviation Systems Service Technician
Aviation Systems Technician
Avionics Electrical Technician (AET)
Avionics Electronics Installer
Avionics Electronics Service Technician
Avionics Electronics Technician
Avionics Installer
Avionics Maintenance Technician
Avionics Service Technician
Avionics Systems Installer
Avionics Systems Integration Manager
Avionics Systems Integration Specialist
Avionics Systems Integration Supervisor
Avionics Systems Maintenance Mechanics
Avionics Systems Service Technician

Avionics Systems Technician
Avionics Technician
Avionics Tester
Bench Technician
Biomedical Electronics Installer
Biomedical Electronics Mechanic
Biomedical Electronics Specialist
Biomedical Electronics Technician
Biomedical Engineering Installer
Biomedical Engineering Mechanic
Biomedical Engineering Specialist
Biomedical Engineering Technician (BMET)
Biomedical Equipment Installer
Biomedical Equipment Mechanic
Biomedical Equipment Specialist
Biomedical Equipment Technician (BMET)
Boat Maintenance Mechanic
Boat Maintenance Service Technician
Boat Maintenance Technician
Boat Mechanic
Boat Rigger
Boat Technician
Brake Maintenance Mechanic
Brake Service Technician
Brake Technician
Bus Engine Maintenance Mechanic
Bus Engine Maintenance Technician
Bus Engine Mechanic
Bus Engine Service Technician
Bus Engine Technician
Bus Maintenance Mechanic
Bus Maintenance Technician
Bus Mechanic
Bus Service Technician
Bus Technician
Cable Technician
Central Office Technician
Certified Biomedical Equipment Technician (CBET)
Certified Data Cabling Installer (CDCI)

Equipment Installation, Maintenance & Repair

Certified Electronics Technician (CET)
Certified Fiber Optics Installer (CFOI)
Certified Professional Data Cabling Installer (CPDCI)
Certified Professional Fiber Optics Installer (CPFOI)
Coin-Operated Machine Installer
Coin-Operated Machine Maintenance Mechanic
Coin-Operated Machine Maintenance Technician
Coin-Operated Machine Service Technician
Coin-Operated Machine Technician
Combination Airframe & Power Plant (A&P) Mechanic
Combination Technician
Communications Technician
Computer Installer
Computer Maintenance Mechanic
Computer Maintenance Technician
Computer Service Technician
Computer Technician
Construction Equipment Maintenance Mechanic
Construction Equipment Maintenance Technician
Construction Equipment Mechanic
Construction Equipment Service Technician
Construction Equipment Technician
Construction Machinery Maintenance Mechanic
Construction Machinery Maintenance Technician
Construction Machinery Mechanic
Construction Machinery Service Technician
Construction Machinery Technician
Copier Machine Installer
Copier Machine Maintenance Mechanic
Copier Machine Maintenance Technician
Copier Machine Service Technician
Copier Machine Technician
Copier Service Technician
Copier Technician
Critical Systems Technician
Custom Bike Builder
Customer Service Engineer
Dialing Equipment Maintenance Technician
Dialing Equipment Technician

Diesel Engine Maintenance Mechanic
Diesel Engine Maintenance Technician
Diesel Engine Mechanic
Diesel Engine Service Technician
Diesel Engine Specialist
Diesel Engine Technician
Diesel Maintenance Mechanic
Diesel Mechanic
Diesel Systems Maintenance Mechanic
Diesel Systems Maintenance Technician
Diesel Systems Mechanic
Diesel Systems Service Technician
Diesel Systems Technician
Diesel Technician
Drivability Technician
Durable Medical Equipment (DME) Installer
Durable Medical Equipment (DME) Mechanic
Durable Medical Equipment (DME) Specialist
Durable Medical Equipment Technician (DME Tech)
Electrical & Instrument Technician (E&I Tech)
Electrical & Instrumentation Manager
Electrical & Instrumentation Supervisor
Electrical Installer
Electrical Maintenance Technician
Electrical Repairman
Electrical Service Technician
Electrical Systems Service Technician
Electrical Systems Technician
Electrical Technician
Electromedical Equipment Installer
Electromedical Equipment Mechanic
Electromedical Equipment Specialist
Electromedical Equipment Technician
Electronic Bench Technician
Electronic Equipment Installer
Electronic Equipment Maintenance Technician
Electronic Equipment Repair Technician
Electronic Equipment Service Technician
Electronic Equipment Technician

Equipment Installation, Maintenance & Repair

Electronic Mechanic
Electronic Technician
Electronics Installer
Electronics Maintenance Technician
Electronics Mechanic
Electronics Repair Technician
Electronics Repair Technician
Electronics Service Technician
Electronics Technician
Engineering Technician
Equipment Maintenance Mechanic
Farm Equipment Mechanic
Farm Vehicle Mechanic
Fax Machine Maintenance Technician
Fax Machine Service Technician
Fax Machine Technician
Field Engineer
Field Mechanic
Field Service Engineer
Field Service Technician
Field Technician
Fleet Mechanic
Forklift Mechanic
Fountain Vending Machine Installer
Fountain Vending Machine Maintenance Mechanic
Fountain Vending Machine Service Technician
Fountain Vending Machine Technician
Fountain Vending Mechanic
Gambling Machine Installer
Gambling Machine Maintenance Mechanic
Gambling Machine Maintenance Technician
Gambling Machine Service Technician
Gambling Technician
Gaming Machine Installer
Gaming Machine Maintenance Mechanic
Gaming Machine Maintenance Technician
Gaming Machine Service Technician
Gaming Technician
Gantry Rigger

Gas Engine Maintenance Mechanic
Gas Engine Maintenance Technician
Gas Engine Mechanic
Gas Engine Service Technician
Gas Engine Technician
Hand Rigger
Harvester Mechanic
Heating Mechanic
Heating Systems Mechanic
Heating Systems Specialist
Heating Systems Technician
Heating Technician
Heavy Duty Mechanic
Heavy Equipment Maintenance Mechanic
Heavy Equipment Maintenance Technician
Heavy Equipment Mechanic
Heavy Equipment Service Technician
Heavy Equipment Technician
Heavy Lift Rigger
Helicopter Maintenance Supervisor
Helicopter Maintenance Technician
Helicopter Mechanic
Helicopter Service Technician
Helicopter Technician
HVAC Installer
HVAC Mechanic
HVAC Specialist
HVAC Technician
HVACR Installer
HVACR Mechanic
HVACR Specialist
HVACR Technician
Industrial Control Systems Maintenance Technician
Industrial Control Systems Service Technician
Industrial Control Systems Technician
Industrial Electrical Systems Maintenance Technician
Industrial Electrical Systems Service Technician
Industrial Electrical Systems Technician
Industrial Electrician

Equipment Installation, Maintenance & Repair

Industrial Electronic Systems Maintenance Technician
Industrial Electronic Systems Service Technician
Industrial Electronic Systems Technician
Industrial Electronics Maintenance Technician
Industrial Electronics Service Technician
Industrial Electronics Technician
Industrial Equipment Installer
Industrial Equipment Mechanic
Industrial Equipment Specialist
Industrial Equipment Technician
Industrial Machinery Installer
Industrial Machinery Mechanic
Industrial Machinery Specialist
Industrial Machinery Technician
Industrial Maintenance Millwright
Industrial Mechanic
Industrial Processing Machinery Installer
Industrial Processing Machinery Mechanic
Industrial Processing Machinery Specialist
Industrial Processing Machinery Technician
Industrial Production Machinery Installer
Industrial Production Machinery Mechanic
Industrial Production Machinery Specialist
Industrial Production Machinery Technician
Industrial Specialist
Industrial Technician
Inspector
Installation & Repair Foreman
Installation & Repair Manager
Installation & Repair Supervisor
Installation & Repair Technician
Installation Foreman
Installation Manager
Installation Supervisor
Installer
Instrument & Electrical Technician (I&E Tech)
Instrumental & Control Technician (I&C Tech)
Journeyman
Journeyman Mechanic

Jukebox Installer
Jukebox Maintenance Mechanic
Jukebox Maintenance Technician
Jukebox Service Technician
Jukebox Technician
Laptop Computer Installer
Laptop Computer Maintenance Mechanic
Laptop Computer Maintenance Technician
Laptop Computer Service Technician
Laptop Computer Technician
Lineman
Machine Adjuster
Machine Repairer
Machinery Erector
Machinery Mover
Mainframe Computer Installer
Mainframe Computer Maintenance Mechanic
Mainframe Computer Maintenance Technician
Mainframe Computer Service Technician
Mainframe Computer Technician
Maintenance Electrician
Maintenance Engineer
Maintenance Foreman
Maintenance Machinist
Maintenance Manager
Maintenance Mechanic
Maintenance Supervisor
Maintenance Technician
Marine Electrician
Marine Mechanic
Marine Propulsion Technician
Marine Rigger
Marine Technician
Master Automotive Technician
Master Mechanic
Master Medium/Heavy Truck Technician
Master School Bus Technician
Master Truck Equipment Technician
Mechanic

Equipment Installation, Maintenance & Repair

Medical Equipment Installer
Medical Equipment Mechanic
Medical Equipment Specialist
Medical Equipment Technician
Medium/Heavy Truck Maintenance Mechanic
Medium/Heavy Truck Mechanic
Meter & Relay Service Technician
Meter & Relay Technician
Meter Service Technician
Mobile Heavy Equipment Maintenance Mechanic
Mobile Heavy Equipment Maintenance Technician
Mobile Heavy Equipment Mechanic
Mobile Heavy Equipment Service Technician
Mobile Heavy Equipment Technician
Mobile Radio Equipment Maintenance Technician
Mobile Radio Equipment Technician
Mobile Radio Receiving Equipment Maintenance Technician
Mobile Radio Receiving Equipment Technician
Mobile Radio Transmitting Equipment Maintenance Technician
Mobile Radio Transmitting Equipment Technician
Motor Vehicle Maintenance Mechanic
Motor Vehicle Maintenance Technician
Motor Vehicle Mechanic
Motor Vehicle Service Technician
Motor Vehicle Technician
Motorboat Mechanic
Motorcycle Maintenance Mechanic
Motorcycle Maintenance Technician
Motorcycle Mechanic
Motorcycle Service Technician
Motorcycle Technician
Motorsports Mechanic
Motorsports Service Technician
Motorsports Technician
Network Equipment Installer
Network Equipment Maintenance Mechanic
Network Equipment Maintenance Technician
Network Equipment Service Technician
Network Equipment Technician

Network Server Installer
Network Server Maintenance Mechanic
Network Server Maintenance Technician
Network Server Service Technician
Network Server Technician
Office Machine Installer
Office Machine Maintenance Mechanic
Office Machine Maintenance Technician
Office Machine Service Technician
Office Machine Technician
Outboard Motor Mechanic
Outboard Technician
Outdoor Power Equipment Mechanic
Outside Plant Technician
Overhauler
Parts Inspector
Peripheral Device Installer
Peripheral Device Maintenance Mechanic
Peripheral Device Maintenance Technician
Peripheral Device Service Technician
Peripheral Device Technician
Personal Computer (PC) Installer
Personal Computer (PC) Maintenance Mechanic
Personal Computer (PC) Maintenance Technician
Personal Computer (PC) Service Technician
Personal Computer (PC) Technician
Photocopier Installer
Photocopier Maintenance Mechanic
Photocopier Maintenance Technician
Photocopier Service Technician
Photocopier Technician
Pipefitter
Pipeline Distribution Systems Installer
Pipeline Distribution Systems Mechanic
Pipeline Distribution Systems Specialist
Pipeline Distribution Systems Technician
Preventive Maintenance Mechanic
Preventive Maintenance Technician
Radio Electronics Installer

Equipment Installation, Maintenance & Repair

Radio Electronics Maintenance Mechanic
Radio Electronics Maintenance Technician
Radio Electronics Service Technician
Radio Electronics Technician
Radio Frequency (RF) Technician
Radio Maintenance Technician
Radio Mechanic
Radio Repairman
Radio Technician
Refinery Systems Installer
Refinery Systems Mechanic
Refinery Systems Specialist
Refinery Systems Technician
Refrigeration Installer
Refrigeration Mechanic
Refrigeration Systems Mechanic
Refrigeration Systems Specialist
Refrigeration Systems Technician
Refrigeration Technician
Relay Service Technician
Relay Technician
Repair Foreman
Repair Manager
Repair Service Technician
Repair Supervisor
Repair Technician
Repairer
Rigger
Rigger Supervisor
Rigging Foreman
Service Mechanic
Service Technician
Ship Rigger
Shop Foreman
Shop Mechanic
Slot Machine Installer
Slot Machine Maintenance Mechanic
Slot Machine Maintenance Technician
Slot Machine Service Technician

Slot Machine Technician
Slot Technician
Small Engine Maintenance Mechanic
Small Engine Maintenance Technician
Small Engine Mechanic
Small Engine Service Technician
Small Engine Technician
Stationary Radio Equipment Maintenance Technician
Stationary Radio Equipment Technician
Stationary Radio Receiving Equipment Maintenance Technician
Stationary Radio Receiving Equipment Technician
Stationary Radio Transmitting Equipment Maintenance Technician
Stationary Radio Transmitting Equipment Technician
Substation Electrician
Substation Maintenance Mechanic
Substation Maintenance Technician
Substation Mechanic
Substation Service Technician
Substation Technician
Surface Mining Equipment Maintenance Mechanic
Surface Mining Equipment Maintenance Technician
Surface Mining Equipment Mechanic
Surface Mining Equipment Service Technician
Surface Mining Equipment Technician
Surface Mining Machinery Maintenance Mechanic
Surface Mining Machinery Maintenance Technician
Surface Mining Machinery Service Technician
Surface Mining Machinery Technician
Switching Equipment Maintenance Technician
Switching Equipment Technician
Telecommunications Equipment Installer
Telecommunications Equipment Maintenance Technician
Telecommunications Equipment Mechanic
Telecommunications Equipment Technician
Telecommunications Line Installer
Telecommunications Line Maintenance Technician
Telecommunications Line Technician
Telecommunications Network Maintenance Technician
Telecommunications Network Technician

Equipment Installation, Maintenance & Repair

Telecommunications Technician
Tractor Engine Maintenance Mechanic
Tractor Engine Maintenance Technician
Tractor Engine Mechanic
Tractor Engine Service Technician
Tractor Engine Technician
Tractor Maintenance Mechanic
Tractor Mechanic
Tractor Service Technician
Tractor Technician
Tractor-Trailer Maintenance Mechanic
Tractor-Trailer Maintenance Technician
Tractor-Trailer Mechanic
Tractor-Trailer Technician
Transit Mechanic
Transportation Maintenance Mechanic
Transportation Mechanic
Trim Technician
Truck Engine Maintenance Mechanic
Truck Engine Maintenance Technician
Truck Engine Mechanic
Truck Engine Service Technician
Truck Engine Technician
Truck Mechanic
Two-Way Radio Technician
Variable Retention Time (VRT) Mechanic
Vehicle Maintenance Mechanic
Vehicle Maintenance Technician
Vehicle Service Technician
Vehicle Technician
Vending Machine Installer
Vending Machine Maintenance Mechanic
Vending Machine Maintenance Technician
Vending Machine Service Technician
Vending Machine Technician
Vending Maintenance Mechanic
Vending Mechanic
Vending Technician
Ventilation Mechanic

Ventilation Systems Mechanic
Ventilation Systems Specialist
Ventilation Systems Technician
Ventilation Technician
Video Game Machine Installer
Video Game Machine Maintenance Mechanic
Video Game Machine Maintenance Technician
Video Game Machine Service Technician
Video Game Machine Technician
Wireman

Equipment Installation, Maintenance & Repair

Software, Systems & Technology

Adobe Acrobat
Adobe Illustrator
AIRPAX
Alliance Automotive Shop Controller Software
Atlas Construction Business Forms
AutoDesk AutoCAD
Automated Inventory Software
AutoZone ALLDATA Software
BIT Corp ProMACS PLC
Building Automation Software
CaseBank SpotLight
Computer-Aided Design & Drafting (CADD) Systems
Computer-Aided Design & Drafting (CADD) Technology
Computer-Aided Design (CAD) Systems
Computer-Aided Design (CAD) Technology
Computerized Aircraft Log Manager (CALM)
Computerized Maintenance Management System (CMMS)
Corel WordPerfect
CynapSys Virtual DER
Data Logging Software
dBase Plus
Engine Analysis Software
Enterprise Resource Planning (ERP) Software
Estimating Software
Facility Energy Management Software
FileMaker Pro
Fleet Management Software
Harris Tech BassBox
Harris Tech X.over Pro
IBM Lotus 1-2-3
IBM Lotus Notes
Installogy
Intuit QuickBooks
Johnson Controls Metasys
KEYENCE PLC Ladder Logic
LinearTeam WinISD

Maintenance Control Software
Maintenance Information Database
Maintenance Management Software
Maintenance Planning & Control Software
Maintenance Planning Software
Maintenance Record Software
Metis Systems MainTrack
Microsoft Access
Microsoft Excel
Microsoft Outlook
Microsoft PowerPoint
Microsoft Project
Microsoft Windows
Microsoft Word
Mitchell Manager Invoicing System
MobileToysMAIDXL
Modular Diagnostic Information Systems
Mxi Technologies Maintenix
Nexiq Tech HDS Suite for Palm
Pentagon 2000SQL
Programmable Logic Controller (PLC)
Proportional Integral Derivative (PID) Controller
S.M.A.R.T. Aircraft Maintenance Tracking
Sacramento Sky Ranch Mechanic's Toolbox
SAP
SAP Maintenance
Shop Management Software
Snap-On ShoKey
SPX/OTC Genisys ConnecTech PC
Structured Query Language (SQL)
Supply System Software
Technical Manual Database Software
True Audio WinSpeakerz
Vehicle Management Software
WHE Term-PAK
WorkTech MAXIMO

KeyWords & KeyWord Phrases for Installation, Maintenance & Repair - Equipment, Machinery, Technology & Vehicles

Adjustable Crescent Wrench
Adjustable Monkey Wrench
Adjustable Wrench
Adjusting
Adjustment
Algebra
Alignment
Alignment Wrench
Ammeter
Analysis Instrumentation
Analysis Instruments
Applied Physics
Apprenticeship
Arbor Press
Arithmetic
Assembly
Association of Communications & Electronics Schools International (ACES)
Ball Peen Hammer
Bearing Puller
Bearings
Bleeder Wrench
Blueprints
Brake Installation
Brake Maintenance
Brake Service
Brake Shoes
Brakes
Brass Hammer
Brass Punch
Brazing
Brazing Equipment
Breakage
Breaker Bar

Buffing
Buffing Machine
Cable
Cable Colors
Cable Winch
Cabling
Calculus
Calibrate
Calibration
Caliper
Center Punch
Chain Wrench
Channel-Lock Pliers
Chemical
Chemistry
Circuit
Circuit Analyzer
Circuit Diagram
Circuit Layouts
Circuitry
Claw Hammer
Cleaning
Clutch
Commercial
Commercial Equipment
Commercial Machinery
Component Configuration
Component-Level Repair
Components
Compression Gauge
Computer Science
Computer-Aided Design & Drafting (CADD)
Computer-Aided Design (CAD)
Computerized Controls
Configuration
Control Cable
Control System
Corrective Maintenance
Crane

Equipment Installation, Maintenance & Repair

Crescent Wrench
Crowfoot Wrench
Customer Service Engineering
Cutting
Cutting Apparatus
Cutting Equipment
Cylindrical Grinder
Data Analysis
Data Collection
Debugging
Defective
Defective Component
Defective Equipment
Defective Materials
Defective Mechanisms
Defective Parts
Defects
Diagnosis
Diagnostic Computer
Diagnostic Instrument
Diagnostic Test
Diagnostic Tool
Diagram
Dial Caliber
Dies
Disassembly
Drawings
Drift
Drill Press
Duct
Electric Power Source
Electrical Circuit
Electrical Component
Electrical Drawings
Electrical Engineering
Electrical Equipment
Electrical Hazards
Electrical Point Settings
Electrical Service

Electrical Test Equipment
Electrical Testing Equipment
Electronic Circuit
Electronic Component
Electronics
Electronics Drawing
Electronics Engineering
Electronics Equipment
Emission Control System
Emissions
Engine
Engine Lathe
Engine Overhaul
Engine Timing
Engine Tuning
Engineering Specifications
Equipment
Equipment Inspection
Equipment Maintenance
Equipment Repair
Excessive Wear
Exhaust
Exhaust Emissions
Exhaust System
Fan
Fault
Fault Analysis
Fault Isolation
Field Engineering
Field Service
Field Service Engineering
Flame-Cutting Equipment
Flare Nut Wrench
Flexible Power Press
Frequency Meter
Fuel Pump
Fuel Pump Test Stand
Fuse
Gas Welder

Equipment Installation, Maintenance & Repair

Gas Welding
Gas Welding Equipment
Gasket
Gasoline Filter
Gauges
Gear Puller Tool
Geometry
Governor Test Stand
Graphing Scanner
Grinder
Grinding Wheel
Hand Tools
Hazardous Materials (HAZMAT)
Heavy Equipment
Hoist
Hose-Clamp Pliers
Hydraulic Engineering
Hydraulic Equipment
Hydraulic Pipe Bender
Hydraulic Squeezer
Hydraulic Test Equipment
Hydraulic Testing Equipment
Hydraulics
Ignition
Ignition System
Industrial Controls
Industrial Engineering
Industrial Equipment
Industrial Machinery
Inside Caliper
Inspection
Inspection Report
Installation
Installation & Repair Management
Installation Management
Installation Procedures
Instrument Maintenance
Instrument Repair
Instrumentation

Instruments
Integrated Maintenance & Inventory Systems
International Association of Machinists & Aerospace Workers (IAMAW)
International Brotherhood of Teamsters (IBT)
Jack
Job Order
Junction Box
Knock-Out Punch
Lathe
Level
Locking C-Clamp Pliers
Locking Pliers
Locking Wrench
Logic
Logical Analysis
Logical Thought
Lubricate
Lubricating
Lubrication
Machine
Machine Adjustment
Machine Attachment
Machine Design
Machine Maintenance
Machine Message Error
Machine Parts
Machine Repair
Machinery
Machinery Design
Machinery Maintenance
Machinery Repair
Magnetic Inspection
Maintenance
Maintenance Check
Maintenance Engineering
Maintenance Logs
Maintenance Machinery
Maintenance Management
Maintenance Manual

Equipment Installation, Maintenance & Repair

Maintenance Procedures
Maintenance Records
Manometer
Manuals
Master Mechanic
Mathematics
Mechanical Components
Mechanical Drawing
Mechanical Engineering
Mechanical Hazards
Mechanical Lifts
Mechanical Overhaul
Mechanical Test Equipment
Mechanical Testing Equipment
Mechanics
Mechanisms
Micrometer
Milling Machine
Monkey Wrench
Motor
Motor Analyzer
Muffler
Multimeter
Nail Set
National Occupational Competency Testing Institute (NOCTI)
National Tooling & Machining Association (NTMA)
Network Configuration
North American Technician Excellence (NATE)
Ohmmeter
Oil
Oil Filter Wrench
Oiler
Operating Manual
Organic Light-Emitting Device
Organic Light-Emitting Display
Oscilloscope
Outside Caliper
Overhaul
Oxyacetylene Welder

Oxyacetylene Welding Equipment
Parts
Parts Inspection
Parts Replacement
Parts Specification
Physical Inspection
Physics
Pin Punch
Pipe Bender
Pipes
Plastic-Tip Hammer
Platform Lift
Pneumatic Engineering
Pneumatic Equipment
Pneumatic Test Equipment
Pneumatic Testing Equipment
Pneumatics
Polishing Machine
Pollution
Pollution Regulations
Polyvinyl Chloride (PVC)
Polyvinyl Chloride (PVC) Bender
Polyvinyl Chloride (PVC) Pipe
Portable Maintenance Access Terminal
Power
Power Buffer
Power Grinder
Power Lifts
Power Source
Power Tools
Precise Instruments
Precision Grinder
Precision Instrumentation
Pressure Gauge
Pressure Indicator
Preventive Maintenance
Pump
Pump Wrench
Punch Press

Equipment Installation, Maintenance & Repair

Punches
Quality
Quality Assurance (QA)
Quality Control (QC)
Quality Management
Radiator
Reassemble
Reassembly
Recordkeeping
Repair
Repair
Repair Management
Repair Procedures
Repair Shop
Replacement Parts
Replacement Parts
Replacement Regulator
Reporting
Retrofit
Routine Maintenance
Safety
Safety Compliance
Safety Regulations
Saw
Scheduled Maintenance
Schematic Drawing
Schematics
Screw Starter
Screwdriver
Seal
Service
Service Bulletin
Service Manual
Service Shop
Sheet Metal
Sheet Metal Breaker
Shop
Shop Mathematics
Signal Generator

Slip Joint Pliers
Slug Wrench
Soft-Face Hammer
Solder
Soldering
Soldering Equipment
Soldering Gun
Soldering Iron
Specialty Wrench
Specifications
Staging Equipment
Starter Punch
Statistical Analysis
Statistics
Steering Control
Structural Drawings
Structural Engineering
Subsystem
Subsystem Assembly
Suspension
Switches
System Configuration
System Overhaul
Tail Pipe
Taper Punch
Taps
Teach Pendant
Team Building
Team Leadership
Technical Drawings
Technical Manual
Technical Specifications
Template
Template Construction
Test
Test Instrumentation
Test Instruments
Test Lamp
Test Meter

Equipment Installation, Maintenance & Repair

Test Operation
Test Reading
Test Signal
Testing
Testing Instrumentation
Testing Instruments
Thermostat
Three-Pin Punch
Throttle
Throttle Control
Tool Design
Tool Maintenance
Tool Repair
Tooling
Tools
Training & Development
Transformer
Troubleshooting
Turning Lathe
United Automobile, Aerospace & Agricultural Implement Workers of America (UAAAIWA)
Vibration
Vibration Analysis
Vise Grip Pliers
Visual Inspection
Vocational School
Vocational Training
Voltage Regulator
Voltmeter
Water Pump
Water Pump Pliers
Wattmeter
Welder
Welding
Welding Equipment
Wheel Bearings
Wheels
Wire Color
Wire Winch

Wiring
Wiring Diagrams
Woodworking Machine
Work Orders
Workflow Planning
Workshop
Workshop Press
Wrench

Equipment Installation, Maintenance & Repair

Additional KeyWords & KeyWord Phrases for Aircraft & Avionics Equipment

Aircraft
Aircraft Assemblies
Aircraft Assembly
Aircraft Electrical Systems
Aircraft Electrical Systems Assembly
Aircraft Electrical Systems Installation
Aircraft Electrical Systems Maintenance
Aircraft Electrical Systems Service
Aircraft Engine
Aircraft Hydraulics
Aircraft Maintenance
Aircraft Maintenance Management Systems
Aircraft Monitoring
Aircraft Monitoring System
Aircraft Repair
Aircraft Service
Aircraft System
Aircraft Test Stands
Airframe
Airframe Assembly
Airframe Maintenance
Airframe Repair
Airframe Service
Aviation Electronics
Aviation Maintenance
Aviation Systems
Aviation Systems Assembly
Aviation Systems Installation
Aviation Systems Maintenance
Aviation Systems Repair
Aviation Systems Service
Avionics
Avionics Assembly
Avionics Assembly
Avionics Electronics

Avionics Electronics Assembly
Avionics Electronics Installation
Avionics Electronics Repair
Avionics Electronics Service
Avionics Installation
Avionics Maintenance
Avionics Management
Avionics Repair
Avionics Service
Avionics Systems
Avionics Systems Assembly
Avionics Systems Installation
Avionics Systems Integration
Avionics Systems Integration Management
Avionics Systems Maintenance
Avionics Systems Repair
Avionics Systems Service
Composite Materials
De-Icer
Federal Aviation Administration (FAA)
Fuel System
Fuselage
Helicopter
Helicopter Assembly
Helicopter Maintenance
Helicopter Repair
Helicopter Service
Hydraulic System
Hydraulic Unit
Hydraulics
In-Flight Refueling System
Instruments
Jet
Landing Gear
Navigation
Navigation System
Navigational System
Offset Left Aviation System
Offset Right Aviation System

Equipment Installation, Maintenance & Repair

Oxygen System
Pneumatic System
Pneumatics
Preflight Check
Pressurization
Pressurized System
Professional Aviation Maintenance Association (PAMA)
Propeller
Propeller-Driven Aircraft
Radar
Radar System
Rigging
Straight-Cut Aviation Snips
Turbine Engine
Weather Radar System
Wings

Additional KeyWords & KeyWord Phrases for Coin, Vending & Amusement Machines

Amusement
Amusement Equipment
Amusement Equipment Assembly
Amusement Equipment Installation
Amusement Equipment Maintenance
Amusement Equipment Repair
Amusement Equipment Service
Amusement Machine
Amusement Machine Assembly
Amusement Machine Installation
Amusement Machine Maintenance
Amusement Machine Repair
Amusement Machine Service
Arcade
Automatic Merchandiser Vending Group (AMVG)
Bill Collection
Bill Validator
Bills
Cash-Operated Machine
Casino
Change-Making Mechanism
Coin Collection
Coin Mechanism
Coin-Operated Machine
Coin-Operated Machine Assembly
Coin-Operated Machine Installation
Coin-Operated Machine Maintenance
Coin-Operated Machine Repair
Coin-Operated Machine Service
Coins
Computerized Inventory Controls
Dispensing
Dispensing Equipment
Electrical Code
Electrical Connection

Equipment Installation, Maintenance & Repair

Fountain Vending Machine
Fountain Vending Machine Assembly
Fountain Vending Machine Installation
Fountain Vending Machine Maintenance
Fountain Vending Machine Repair
Fountain Vending Machine Service
Gambling Machine
Gambling Machine Assembly
Gambling Machine Installation
Gambling Machine Maintenance
Gambling Machine Repair
Gambling Machine Service
Gaming Machine
Gaming Machine Assembly
Gaming Machine Installation
Gaming Machine Maintenance
Gaming Machine Repair
Gaming Machine Service
Joystick
Jukebox
Jukebox Assembly
Jukebox Installation
Jukebox Maintenance
Jukebox Repair
Jukebox Service
Keypad
Merchandise Chute
Microwave
Microwave Oven
Microwave Technology
Money
Money Collection
National Automatic Merchandising Association (NAMA)
Pinball Machine
Plumbing Code
Product Inventory
Product Management
Product Replenishment
Products

Public Health Regulations
Public Health Standards
Sanitation Regulations
Sanitation Standards
Slot Machine
Slot Machine Assembly
Slot Machine Installation
Slot Machine Maintenance
Slot Machine Repair
Slot Machine Service
Vending
Vending Machine
Vending Machine Assembly
Vending Machine Installation
Vending Machine Maintenance
Vending Machine Repair
Vending Machine Service
Vending Service
Video Game Machine
Video Game Machine Assembly
Video Game Machine Installation
Video Game Machine Maintenance
Video Game Machine Repair
Video Game Machine Service
Water
Water Connection
Water Supply

Additional KeyWords & KeyWord Phrases for Computer, ATM & Office Machines

Automated Teller Machine (ATM)
Automated Teller Machine (ATM) Assembly
Automated Teller Machine (ATM) Installation
Automated Teller Machine (ATM) Maintenance
Automated Teller Machine (ATM) Repair
Automated Teller Machine (ATM) Service
Back-Up
Banking
Cables
Cabling
Cash Register
Communication Link
Communications
Computer
Computer Assembly
Computer Installation
Computer Maintenance
Computer Repair
Computer Service
Copier
Copier Machine
Copier Machine Assembly
Copier Machine Installation
Copier Machine Maintenance
Copier Machine Repair
Copier Machine Service
Disk Drive
Duplicating Machine
Electronic Equipment
Electronic Equipment Installation
Electronic Equipment Maintenance
Electronic Equipment Repair
Electronic Equipment Service
Electronics
Electronics Repair

Finding Needles in a Haystack

Electronics Service
Fax
Fax Machine
Fax Machine Assembly
Fax Machine Installation
Fax Machine Maintenance
Fax Machine Repair
Fax Machine Service
Flash Drive
Hard Drive
Laptop Computer
Laptop Computer Assembly
Laptop Computer Installation
Laptop Computer Maintenance
Laptop Computer Repair
Laptop Computer Service
Mail-Processing Equipment
Mainframe
Mainframe Computer
Mainframe Computer Assembly
Mainframe Computer Installation
Mainframe Computer Maintenance
Mainframe Computer Repair
Mainframe Computer Service
Network Analyzer
Network Card
Network Equipment
Network Equipment Assembly
Network Equipment Installation
Network Equipment Maintenance
Network Equipment Repair
Network Equipment Service
Network Server
Network Server Assembly
Network Server Installation
Network Server Maintenance
Network Server Repair
Network Server Service
Office Machine Assembly

Equipment Installation, Maintenance & Repair

Office Machine Installation
Office Machine Maintenance
Office Machine Repair
Office Machine Service
Office Machine
Operating Software
Operating System
Peripheral Device
Peripheral Device Assembly
Peripheral Device Installation
Peripheral Device Maintenance
Peripheral Device Repair
Peripheral Device Service
Peripheral Equipment
Personal Computer (PC)
Personal Computer (PC) Computer Assembly
Personal Computer (PC) Installation
Personal Computer (PC) Maintenance
Personal Computer (PC) Repair
Personal Computer (PC) Service
Photocopier
Photocopier Assembly
Photocopier Installation
Photocopier Maintenance
Photocopier Repair
Photocopier Service
Printer
Server
System Back-Up
Transaction Processing
Video Card

Additional KeyWords & KeyWord Phrases for Electrical & Electronic Systems, Equipment & Machines

Alarm
Alarm System
Amperage
Amps
Antennae
Antennas
Automated Electronic Control System
Capacitance
Circuit
Circuit Board
Circuitry
Communication Link
Communications
Current
Electric Generating Plant
Electric Motor
Electric Pump
Electric Switch
Electric System
Electrical Equipment
Electrical Maintenance
Electrical Repair
Electrical Systems
Electrical Systems Assembly
Electrical Systems Maintenance
Electricity
Electronic Equipment
Electronic Equipment Installation
Electronic Equipment Maintenance
Electronic Equipment Repair
Electronic Equipment Service
Electronic Navigation Equipment
Electronic Security Equipment
Electronic Sensor

Equipment Installation, Maintenance & Repair

Electronic Sonar Equipment
Electronic Sound Equipment
Electronic Surveillance Equipment
Electronic System Assembly
Electronics
Electronics Assembly
Electronics Maintenance
Electronics Repair
Electronics Service
Electronics Technicians Association International (ETAI)
Gain
Generating Plant
Generating Substation
High Voltage
High-Voltage Detection
High-Voltage Detector
Inductance
Industrial Control Systems
Industrial Control Systems Assembly
Industrial Control Systems Maintenance
Industrial Control Systems Repair
Industrial Control Systems Service
Industrial Controls
Industrial Electrical Systems
Industrial Electrical Systems Assembly
Industrial Electrical Systems Maintenance
Industrial Electrical Systems Repair
Industrial Electrical Systems Service
Industrial Electronic Systems
Industrial Electronic Systems Assembly
Industrial Electronic Systems Maintenance
Industrial Electronic Systems Repair
Industrial Electronic Systems Service
Industrial Electronics
Industrial Electronics Assembly
Industrial Electronics Maintenance
Industrial Electronics Repair
Industrial Electronics Service
In-Service Relay

Insulation
Insulation Loss
Integrated Circuit Board (ICB)
International Society of Certified Electronics Technicians (ISCET)
Low Voltage
Low-Voltage Detection
Low-Voltage Detector
Meter & Relay Service
Meter Maintenance
Meter Service
Missile Control System
Motor
Navigation System
Nuclear
Nuclear Generating Plant
Polarity
Polarity Tester
Power
Power Source
Power Transformer
Programmable Logic Control (PLC)
Pumps
Radar
Radio Electronics
Radio Electronics Installation
Radio Electronics Maintenance
Radio Electronics Repair
Radio Electronics Service
Relay
Relay Service
Resistance
Satellite Navigation System
Security System
Sensor
Signal
Signal Transmission
Sonar System
Sound System
Substation

Equipment Installation, Maintenance & Repair

Substation Control System
Substation Maintenance
Substation Relay System
Substation Repair
Substation Service
Surveillance System
Switches
Transformer
Transistor
Transmitter
Volt
Voltage
Watertight
Watertight Electrical Equipment
Watertight Electrical System
Watertight Electronic Equipment
Watertight Electronic System
Wattage
Watts

Additional KeyWords & KeyWord Phrases for Farm Equipment & Machinery

Agricultural Equipment
Agricultural Machinery
Baler
Combine
Dairy Equipment
Dairy Machinery
Farm Equipment
Farm Machinery
Farm Vehicle
Harvester
Irrigation Systems
Tractor
Tractor Assembly
Tractor Engine
Tractor Engine Assembly
Tractor Engine Maintenance
Tractor Engine Repair
Tractor Engine Service
Tractor Maintenance
Tractor Mechanic
Tractor Service

Additional KeyWords & KeyWord Phrases for Heating, Ventilating, Air Conditioning & Refrigeration Systems

Acetylene Torch
Air Conditioning
Air Conditioning & Refrigeration Institute (ARI)
Air Conditioning & Refrigeration Safety Coalition (ACRSC)
Air Conditioning Contractors of America (ACCA)
Air Conditioning Systems
Air Conditioning Systems Installation
Air Conditioning Systems Maintenance
Air Conditioning Systems Repair
Air Conditioning Systems Service
Air Flow Hood
Air Quality
Alternating Current (AC) Line Splitter
Associated Builders & Contractors (ABC)
Bead-Type Thermocouple
Bourdon Tube
Bubble Level
Burner
Burner Nozzle
Carbon Dioxide Tester
Carbon Monoxide Safety Association (CMSA)
Carbon Monoxide Tester
Chlorofluorocarbon (CFC)
Climate Control
Combustion Analyzer
Combustion Test Equipment
Commercial
Condenser
Condensing Unit
Current Meter
Ductwork
Environmental Protection Agency (EPA)
Evaporator
Flow Meter

Flow Sensors
Gas Pressure Gauge
Hazardous Coolants
Heating Systems
Heating Systems Installation
Heating Systems Maintenance
Heating Systems Repair
Heating Systems Service
Heating, Ventilating & Air Conditioning Systems (HVAC)
Heating, Ventilating, Air Conditioning & Refrigeration Systems (HVACR)
Home Builders Institute (HBI)
HVAC Installation
HVAC Maintenance
HVAC Repair
HVAC Service
HVACR Installation
HVACR Maintenance
HVACR Repair
HVACR Service
Hydrochlorofluorocarbon (HCFC)
Hydrofluorocarbon (HFC)
Hydronics
Industrial
Laser Level
Leak
Leak Detection
Leak Isolation
Leak Repair
Leakage
Magnehelic Gauge
Mechanical Contractors Association of America (MCAA)
National Association of Home Builders (NAHB)
National Center for Construction Education & Research (NCCER)
Non-Contact Voltage Detector
of the US and Canada
Oxygen Tester
Partnership for Air Conditioning, Heating & Refrigeration Accreditation (PHARA)
Pilot Tube

Equipment Installation, Maintenance & Repair

Pipe
Pipe Clamp Thermocouple
Pipe Cutting
Pipe Fitting
Pipe Installation
Pipe Joint
Pipe Maintenance
Pipe Repair
Piping
Plumbing-Heating-Cooling Contractors (PHCC)
Pneumatic Air Gauge
Precision Level
Pressure
Pressure Gauge
Pressure Indicator
Pressure Measurement
Pressure Simulator
Refrigerant
Refrigerant Pressure
Refrigerant Pressure Meter
Refrigerant Reclaiming
Refrigeration
Refrigeration Line
Refrigeration Service Engineers Society (RSES)
Refrigeration Systems
Refrigeration Systems Installation
Refrigeration Systems Maintenance
Refrigeration Systems Repair
Refrigeration Systems Service
Residential
Sheet Metal & Air Conditioning Contractors National Association (SMACNA)
Sheet Metal Workers' International Association (SMWIA)
Soft Face Hammer
Solar Energy
Solar Panels
Solar Power
Temperature
Temperature Adjustment

Temperature Gauge
Thermocouple
Thermometer
Tinners Hammer
Tube
Tube Cutter
Tubing
Tubing Joint
Tubing Maintenance
Tubing Repair
Turbine Flow Meter
United Association of Journeymen & Apprentices of the Plumbing & Pipefitting Industry
Ventilating Systems
Ventilation
Ventilation Systems
Ventilation Systems Installation
Ventilation Systems Maintenance
Ventilation Systems Repair
Ventilation Systems Service
Venturi Meter
Voltage Detector
Voltage Meter
Water Flow Meter
Water Level
Water Pressure Gauge
Water Temperature Gauge

Additional KeyWords & KeyWord Phrases for Industrial Equipment & Machinery

Industrial
Industrial Control
Industrial Control Equipment
Industrial Control Software
Industrial Control System
Industrial Equipment
Industrial Equipment Installation
Industrial Equipment Maintenance
Industrial Equipment Repair
Industrial Equipment Service
Industrial Installation
Industrial Machinery Installation
Industrial Machinery Maintenance
Industrial Machinery Repair
Industrial Machinery Service
Industrial Maintenance
Industrial Processing Machinery
Industrial Processing Machinery Installation
Industrial Processing Machinery Maintenance
Industrial Processing Machinery Repair
Industrial Processing Machinery Service
Industrial Production Machinery
Industrial Production Machinery Installation
Industrial Production Machinery Maintenance
Industrial Production Machinery Repair
Industrial Production Machinery Service
Industrial Repair
Industrial Service
Industry
Industry Machinery
Pipeline Distribution Systems
Pipeline Distribution Systems Installation
Pipeline Distribution Systems Maintenance
Pipeline Distribution Systems Repair
Pipeline Distribution Systems Service

Refinery Systems
Refinery Systems Installation
Refinery Systems Maintenance
Refinery Systems Repair
Refinery Systems Service

Additional KeyWords & KeyWord Phrases for Medical Equipment & Technology

Biomedical Electronics
Biomedical Electronics Installation
Biomedical Electronics Maintenance
Biomedical Electronics Repair
Biomedical Electronics Service
Biomedical Engineering
Biomedical Engineering Installation
Biomedical Engineering Maintenance
Biomedical Engineering Repair
Biomedical Engineering Service
Biomedical Equipment
Biomedical Equipment Installation
Biomedical Equipment Maintenance
Biomedical Equipment Repair
Biomedical Equipment Service
Durable Medical Equipment (DME)
Durable Medical Equipment (DME) Installation
Durable Medical Equipment (DME) Maintenance
Durable Medical Equipment (DME) Repair
Durable Medical Equipment (DME) Service
Electromedical
Electromedical Equipment
Electromedical Equipment Installation
Electromedical Equipment Maintenance
Electromedical Equipment Repair
Electromedical Equipment Service
Medical Equipment
Medical Equipment Installation
Medical Equipment Maintenance
Medical Equipment Repair
Medical Equipment Service
Medical Equipment Technology
Medical Technology

Additional KeyWords & KeyWord Phrases for Radio & Telecommunications Equipment

Amplification
Amplifier
Audio
Audio Signal
Audio Visual (AV) Electronic Equipment
Audio Visual (AV) Electronic Receiving Equipment
Audio Visual (AV) Electronic Reception Equipment
Audio Visual (AV) Electronic Transmission Equipment
Audio Visual (AV) Electronic Transmitting Equipment
Broadcasting
Cable Splicer
Cables
Cabling
Capacity
Cell Phone
Cell Tower
Cellular Communications
Central Hub
Central Office
Central Office Communications
Circuit Board
Circuitry
Circuits
Communication Link
Communications
Communications Transmission
Conductor
Conduit
Data Signal
Data Transfer
Data Transfer Rate
Data Transmission
Dialing Equipment
Dialing Equipment Installation
Dialing Equipment Maintenance

Equipment Installation, Maintenance & Repair

Dialing Equipment Repair
Dialing Equipment Service
Dialing Equipment Set Up
Digital Subscriber Line (DSL)
Federal Communications Commission (FCC)
Fiber Optic Communications
Fiber Optic Line
Fiber Optic Technology
Fiber Optics
High-Speed Communications
Inbound Communications
Incoming Communications
Integrated Circuits
Internet
Internet Access
Internet Configuration
Intranet
Intranet Access
Intranet Configuration
Line Installation
Message
Message Transmission
Messaging
Mobile Radio
Mobile Radio Equipment
Mobile Radio Equipment Assembly
Mobile Radio Equipment Installation
Mobile Radio Equipment Maintenance
Mobile Radio Equipment Repair
Mobile Radio Equipment Service
Mobile Radio Receiving Equipment
Mobile Radio Receiving Equipment Assembly
Mobile Radio Receiving Equipment Installation
Mobile Radio Receiving Equipment Maintenance
Mobile Radio Receiving Equipment Repair
Mobile Radio Receiving Equipment Service
Mobile Radio Transmitting Equipment
Mobile Radio Transmitting Equipment Assembly
Mobile Radio Transmitting Equipment Installation

Mobile Radio Transmitting Equipment Maintenance
Mobile Radio Transmitting Equipment Repair
Mobile Radio Transmitting Equipment Service
Moisture
Moisture-Proof Covering
Network
Network Analyzer
Network Applications
Network Operations
Optical
Optical Switching
Outbound Communications
Outgoing Communications
Packet
Packet Switching
Polarity Probe
Power Lines
Private Branch Exchange (PBX)
Radio
Radio Assembly
Radio Installation
Radio Maintenance
Radio Repair
Radio Signal
Radio Signal Transmission
Radio Transmission
Relay Signal
Repeater
Resister
Router
Routing
Satellite
Satellite Communications
Semiconductor
Signal
Signal Delay
Signal Interference
Signal Quality
Signal Strength

Equipment Installation, Maintenance & Repair

Signal Transmission
Society of Cable Telecommunications Engineers (SCTE)
Software
Software Installation
Splice
Splicing
Stationary Radio
Stationary Radio Equipment
Stationary Radio Equipment Assembly
Stationary Radio Equipment Installation
Stationary Radio Equipment Maintenance
Stationary Radio Equipment Repair
Stationary Radio Equipment Service
Stationary Radio Receiving Equipment
Stationary Radio Receiving Equipment Assembly
Stationary Radio Receiving Equipment Installation
Stationary Radio Receiving Equipment Maintenance
Stationary Radio Receiving Equipment Repair
Stationary Radio Receiving Equipment Service
Stationary Radio Transmitting Equipment
Stationary Radio Transmitting Equipment Assembly
Stationary Radio Transmitting Equipment Installation
Stationary Radio Transmitting Equipment Maintenance
Stationary Radio Transmitting Equipment Repair
Stationary Radio Transmitting Equipment Service
String Lines
Switchboard
Switches
Switching Equipment
Switching Equipment Installation
Switching Equipment Maintenance
Switching Equipment Repair
Switching Equipment Service
Switching Equipment Set Up
Switching Station
Telecommunications
Telecommunications Network Installation
Telecommunications Equipment
Telecommunications Equipment

Telecommunications Equipment Assembly
Telecommunications Equipment Installation
Telecommunications Equipment Maintenance
Telecommunications Equipment Repair
Telecommunications Equipment Service
Telecommunications Line
Telecommunications Line Assembly
Telecommunications Line Installation
Telecommunications Line Maintenance
Telecommunications Line Repair
Telecommunications Line Service
Telecommunications Lines
Telecommunications Network
Telecommunications Network Assembly
Telecommunications Network Maintenance
Telecommunications Network Repair
Telecommunications Network Service
Telecommunications Wiring
Telephone
Telephone Cables
Telephone Cabling
Telephone Jack
Telephone Wiring
Television Cable
Tension
Terminal
Terminal Box
Tower
Transmission
Transmission Capacity
Transmission Characteristics
Transmission Tower
Transmitter
Two-Way Radio
Two-Way Radio Assembly
Two-Way Radio Communications
Two-Way Radio Installation
Two-Way Radio Maintenance
Two-Way Radio Repair

Equipment Installation, Maintenance & Repair

Two-Way Radio Service
Underground Cable
Underground Cabling
Utilities
Utility Poles
Video on Demand
Voice Over Internet Protocol (VoIP)
Voice Signal
Voice Transmission
Wireless
Wireless Communications
Wireless System

Additional KeyWords & KeyWord Phrases for Rigging

Cable
Chain Fall
Chain Hoist
Construction
Construction Project
Gallow Frame
Gantry
Gin Pole
Hand Rigging
Heavy Lift Rigging
Hoisting
Industrial
Industrial Plant
Load Size
Load Weight
Loads
Logging Yard
Machinery
Machinery Alignment
Machinery Anchor
Machinery Erection
Machinery Moving
Manufacturing
Manufacturing Plant
Marine Rigging
Moving
Multi-Point Suspension
Pulley
Pulling Gear
Rigging
Rigging Lines
Rigging Maintenance
Rigging Repair
Rigging Set Up
Ship Rigging

Equipment Installation, Maintenance & Repair

Shipyard
Winch

Additional KeyWords & KeyWord Phrases for Vehicular Systems - Automotive, Motorboat, Motorcycle, Heavy Equipment, Small Engine & Diesel

Air Bags
All Terrain Vehicle (ATV)
All Terrain Vehicle (ATV) Assembly
All Terrain Vehicle (ATV) Maintenance
All Terrain Vehicle (ATV) Repair
All Terrain Vehicle (ATV) Service
Amalgamated Transit Union (ATU)
Anti-Lock Braking System (ABS)
Association of Diesel Specialists (ADS)
Auto Scanner
Automobile
Automotive
Automotive Assembly
Automotive Engine
Automotive Maintenance
Automotive Repair
Automotive Service
Automotive Service Excellence (ASE)
Backhoe
Ball Joint
Ball Joint Separator
Bearings
Bilge Pump
Boat
Boat Assembly
Boat Engine
Boat Maintenance
Boat Repair
Boat Service
Brake Systems
Brakes
Bulldozer
Bus

Equipment Installation, Maintenance & Repair

Bus Assembly
Bus Engine
Bus Engine Assembly
Bus Engine Maintenance
Bus Engine Repair
Bus Engine Service
Bus Maintenance
Bus Repair
Bus Service
Carburetor
Carburetor Mixture
Chain Saw
Combine
Computerized Engine Analyzer
Construction Equipment
Construction Equipment Assembly
Construction Equipment Maintenance
Construction Equipment Repair
Construction Equipment Service
Construction Machinery
Construction Machinery Assembly
Construction Machinery Maintenance
Construction Machinery Repair
Construction Machinery Service
Conveyor
Crane
Crawler-Loader
Cylinder
Cylinder Head
Detroit Diesel Electronic Control (DDEC) Reader
Diesel Engine
Diesel Engine Assembly
Diesel Engine Maintenance
Diesel Engine Repair
Diesel Engine Service
Diesel Systems
Diesel Systems Maintenance
Diesel Systems Repair
Diesel Systems Service

Finding Needles in a Haystack

Dirt Bike
Distributor
Drive Train
Dynamometer
Electrical Systems
Electronic Systems
Emissions
Emissions Catalyst
Emissions Filter
Emissions Standards
Exhaust System
Farm Combine
Farm Tractor
Feeler Gauges
Fleet
Fleet Maintenance
Fleet Management
Fleet Repair
Fork
Four-Stroke Engine
Front-End Loader
Fuel
Fuel Injection System
Fuel System
Fuel Timing
Fueling System
Gas
Gas Engine
Gas Engine Assembly
Gas Engine Maintenance
Gas Engine Repair
Gas Engine Service
Gas Tank
Gasoline-Powered Equipment
Gears
Generator
Generator Output
Grader
Handlebar

Equipment Installation, Maintenance & Repair

Handlebar Controls
Headlights
Heavy Duty
Heavy Equipment
Heavy Equipment Assembly
Heavy Equipment Maintenance
Heavy Equipment Repair
Heavy Vehicle
Horn
Hydraulics
Ignition
Ignition Timing
Inboard Boat Engine
Lawn Mower
Logging Equipment
Logging Machinery
Lubrication
Magnetos
Mobile Equipment
Mobile Heavy Equipment
Mobile Heavy Equipment Assembly
Mobile Heavy Equipment Maintenance
Mobile Heavy Equipment Repair
Mobile Heavy Equipment Service
Moped
Motor Vehicle
Motor Vehicle Assembly
Motor Vehicle Maintenance
Motor Vehicle Repair
Motor Vehicle Service
Motor Vehicle Technician
Motorcycle
Motorcycle Assembly
Motorcycle Maintenance
Motorcycle Repair
Motorcycle Service
Muffler
National Institute for Automotive Service Excellent (ASE)
Oil Tank

Outboard Boat Engine
Outdoor Power Equipment
Pistons
Points
Power Tilt
Propeller
Propeller Shaft
Railcar
Rings
Road Grader
Scooter
Scooter Assembly
Scooter Maintenance
Scooter Repair
Scooter Service
Small Engine
Small Engine Assembly
Small Engine Maintenance
Small Engine Repair
Small Engine Service
Spark Plug Caps
Spark Plugs
Starter
Steering Mechanisms
Steering Systems
Subassemblies
Surface Mining Equipment
Surface Mining Equipment Assembly
Surface Mining Equipment Maintenance
Surface Mining Equipment Repair
Surface Mining Equipment Service
Surface Mining Machinery
Surface Mining Machinery Assembly
Surface Mining Machinery Repair
Surface Mining Machinery Service
Suspension
Tachometer
Tractor
Tractor Engine

Equipment Installation, Maintenance & Repair

Tractor Engine Assembly
Tractor Engine Maintenance
Tractor Engine Repair
Tractor Engine Service
Tractor-Trailer
Tractor-Trailer Assembly
Tractor-Trailer Maintenance
Tractor-Trailer Repair
Tractor-Trailer Service
Transit
Transit Systems
Transit Workers Union of America (TWUA)
Transmission
Transportation
Trim
Truck Assembly
Truck Engine
Truck Engine Assembly
Truck Engine Maintenance
Truck Engine Repair
Truck Engine Service
Two-Stroke Engine
Undercarriage
Valves
Vehicle
Vehicle Assembly
Vehicle Frame
Vehicle Maintenance
Vehicle Repair
Vehicle Service
Water Pump
Wheel Bearings
Wheels

Add Your Own Keywords & Keyword Phrases

Chapter 8

Hazardous Materials

Principal Keyword List:

Hazardous Materials

Representative Job Titles

Asbestos Abatement Manager
Asbestos Abatement Specialist
Biological Remediation Specialist
Biological Remediation Technician
Chemical Remediation Specialist
Chemical Remediation Technician
Decontamination & Decommissioning Operator (D&D Operator)
Hazardous Materials (HAZMAT) Driver
Hazardous Materials (HAZMAT) Engineer
Hazardous Materials (HAZMAT) Engineering Technician
Hazardous Materials (HAZMAT) Field Engineer
Hazardous Materials (HAZMAT) Field Technician
Hazardous Materials (HAZMAT) Handler
Hazardous Materials (HAZMAT) Removal Worker
Hazardous Materials (HAZMAT) Specialist
Hazardous Materials (HAZMAT) Technician
Inspector
Nuclear Remediation Specialist
Nuclear Remediation Technician
Nuclear Waste Technician
Radiological Control & Safety Technician
Radiological Control Technician
Radiological Remediation Specialist
Remediation Manager
Remediation Officer
Remediation Specialist
Safety Officer
Safety Technician
Site Remediation Manager
Waste Handling Technician
Waste Remediation Specialist
Waste Remediation Technician
Wastewater Remediation Specialist
Wastewater Remediation Technician

Software, Systems & Technology

3-D Scanning Software
Adobe Acrobat
Analytical Software
Bill of Materials Software
Cost Estimating Software
Database Query Software
Database Software
Defect Tracking Software
Document Management Software
Failure Mode & Effects Analysis (FEMA) Software
FileMaker Pro
Fire Safety Inspection & Testing Software
Geomechanical Design Analysis (GDA) Software
Graphics Software
Hazardous Waste Operations & Emergency Response Standard (HAZWOPER) Training Software
IBM Lotus 1-2-3
IBM Lotus Notes
Incident Tracking Software
Instrument Control Software
Intuit QuickBooks
JD Edwards EnterpriseOne Project Management
Laboratory Information Management System (LIMS)
Material Safety Data Sheet (MSDS) Software
Materials Requirements Planning (MRP) Software)
Mathworks MATLAB
Microsoft Access
Microsoft Excel
Microsoft Outlook
Microsoft PowerPoint
Microsoft Project
Microsoft Windows
Microsoft Word
Network Flow Modeling Software
Operation Respond Emergency Information System (OREISTM)
Presentation Software

Project Analysis & Costing Software
Requirements Management Software
Robotic Control Software
Safety Integrity Level (SIL) Software
Safety, Health & Environmental Management Software
Scientific Softwaer
Site Manager
Site Remediation Management Software
Spreadsheet Software
Statistical Analysis Software
Statistical Software
Waste Management Software

KeyWords & KeyWord Phrases for Hazardous Materials

Search Tip: The words "Hazardous Materials" and "HAZMAT" can be used interchangeably.

Abatement
Aerosol Meter
Air
Air Contaminant
Air Contamination
Air Monitor
Air Monitoring Equipment
Air Monitoring Technology
Air Sampling Equipment
Air Sampling Technology
Airborne Particles
Alpha Radiation Meter
Asbestos
Asbestos Abatement
Beta Radiation Meter
Biological
Biological Contaminant
Biological Contamination
Biological HAZMAT
Chemical
Chemical Composition
Chemical Contaminant
Chemical HAZMAT
Chemical Properties
Chemical Structure
Contaminant
Contaminated Air
Contaminated Soil
Contaminated Substance
Contaminated Waste
Contamination
Crisis Management
Crisis Response

Decommissioning
Decontamination
Decontamination & Decommissioning Operations
Detergent
Disaster Response
Disposal
Disposal Method
Disposal Site
Dosimeter
Earth-Moving Equipment
Electric Power Plant
Emergency Planning
Emergency Preparedness
Emergency Response
Environmental Protection Agency (EPA)
Federal Laws
Filter Pump
Forklift
Fuel
Fuel Element
Fuel Waste
Groundwater
Groundwater Sampling
Groundwater Sampling Equipment
Groundwater Sampling Technology
Hazardous Materials (HAZMAT)
Hazardous Materials (HAZMAT) Disposal
Hazardous Materials (HAZMAT) Identification
Hazardous Materials (HAZMAT) Packaging
Hazardous Materials (HAZMAT) Remediation
Hazardous Materials (HAZMAT) Removal
Hazardous Materials (HAZMAT) Transportation
Hazardous Waste
Health Hazards
Incineration
Incinerator Facility
Industrial Furnace
Irradiated Element
Irradiation

Landfill
Lead
Lead Contaminant
Lead-Based Paint
Liquid Splash
Liquid Splash Protective Clothing
Measurement
Mold
Mold Remediation
Nuclear
Nuclear Contaminants
Nuclear Contamination
Nuclear Facilities
Nuclear HAZMAT
Nuclear Regulatory Commission (NRC)
Nuclear Remediation
Nuclear Waste
Personal Air Monitor
Personal Air Monitoring Equipment
Personal Air Monitoring Technology
Personal Protection Equipment
Personal Protective Suits
Pneumatic Scabbing Tool
Protection
Protective Clothing
Public Affairs
Public Hazard
Public Health
Public Safety
Pump
Radiation
Radiation Meter
Radiation Survey Meter
Radiation-Protection Equipment
Radioactive Material
Radiological Remediation
Regulations
Regulatory Affairs
Regulatory Inspection

Regulatory Reporting
Remediation
Remediation Management
Remediation Operations
Respiration
Respiration Equipment
Risk
Risk Assessment
Risk Identification
Risk Management
Risk Mediation
Safety
Safety Equipment
Safety Procedures
Safety Technology
Sandblaster
Self-Contained Protective Suit
Site
Site Contaminants
Site Contamination
Site Management
Site Remediation
Site Safety
Slurry
Slurry Blast Equipment
Soil
Soil Contaminants
Soil Contamination
Soil Remediation
Solvents
Steam Cleaners
Steel Shot Recyclable Blasting Equipment
Surface Particles
Thermoluminescent Dosimeter
Transportation
Treatment
Vapor
Vapor Protective Garment
Waste

Hazardous Materials

Waste Disposal
Waste Handling
Waste Management
Waste Oil
Wastewater
Wastewater Contaminants
Wastewater Contamination
Wastewater Management
Wastewater Remediation
Wastewater Sampling
Wastewater Sampling Kit
Wastewater Sampling Pump
Water
Water Contaminants
Water Contamination
Water Remediation
Water Sampling
Water Sampling Kit
Water Sampling Pump

Add Your Own Keywords & Keyword Phrases

Chapter 9

Manufacturing Production & Operations

Principal Keyword List:

Principal Manufacturing & Production Industries
Manufacturing Production Operations

Additional Keyword Lists:

Aircraft Structure, Surface, Rigging & Systems Assembly
Chemical Plant Operations
Coating, Painting, Plating & Spraying Machine Operations
Crane & Tower Operations
Crushing, Grinding & Polishing Machine Operations
Dredging, Excavating & Loading Equipment Operations
Electrical & Electronic Equipment Assembly
Engine & Other Machines Assembly
Extruding, Forming, Pressing & Compacting Machine Operations
Farming & Agriculture Machine & Equipment Operations
Forging Machine & Foundry Operations
Furnace, Kiln, Oven, Drier & Kettle Operations
Gas Plant & Gas Compressor Operations
Logging Equipment & Machine Operations
Machine & Equipment Operations (General)
Machine Tool & Computer-Controlled Machine Tool Operations
Medical, Dental & Ophthalmic Laboratory Operations
Metal Refining Operations
Mixing & Blending Operations
Photographic Processing Machine & Equipment Operations
Power Plant Operations & Distribution
Printing Machine Operations
Quality & Inspection
Rolling Machine Operations
Saw Machine Operations
Stationary Engineering, Boiler & Heating Equipment Operations
Tool & Die Making
Water & Liquid Waste Treatment Plant Operations

Representative Job Titles

Accredited Farm Manager (AFM)
Agricultural Equipment Operator
Agricultural Machinery Operator
Agricultural Manager
Aircraft Engine Assembler
Aircraft Engine Builder
Aircraft Engine Installer
Aircraft Engine Technician
Aircraft Line Assembler
Aircraft Structural Assembler
Aircraft Systems Assembler
Aircraft Systems Installer
Airframe Assembler
Airframe Structural Assembler
Airframe Structure Installer
Airframe Systems Assembler
Airframe Systems Installer
Airplane Assembler
Airplane Engine Assembler
Airplane Engine Builder
Airplane Engine Installer
Airplane Engine Technician
Airplane Line Assembler
Airplane Structural Assembler
Airplane Systems Assembler
Airplane Systems Installer
Anodizing Line Operator
Aquaculture Manager
Area Plant Manager
Area Plant Operations Manager
Area Production Manager
Area Production Operations Manager
Armature Assembler
Armature Installer
Assembler
Assembly Manager

Manufacturing Production & Operations

Assembly Supervisor
Assembly Technician
Assembly Worker
Assistant Manufacturing Manager
Assistant Operations Manager
Assistant Plant Manager
Assistant Production Manager
Automatic Furnace Operator
Automotive Engine Assembler
Automotive Engine Builder
Automotive Engine Installer
Automotive Engine Technician
Auxiliary Operator
Aviation Systems Assembler
Aviation Systems Installer
Backhoe Operator
Backup Saw Operator
Backup Sawyer
Baler Operator
Band Saw Operator
Band Sawyer
Batch Heat Treat Operator
Batch Operator
Beveller Operator
Blacksmith
Blending Machine Operator
Boiler Engineer
Boiler Operations Manager
Boiler Operator
Brake Press Operator
Breakdown Mill Operator
Breaker Unit Assembler
Breaker Unit Installer
Buffing Machine Operator
Bulkhead Assembly
Bulkhead Installer
Calciner Operator
Calender Operator
Cell Operator

Centerless Grinder Operator
Central Melt Specialist
Chemical Operator
Chemical Plant Operations Technician
Chemical Plant Operator
Chemical Plant Tender
Chemical Processor
Circular Saw Operator
Circular Sawyer
Coater Associate
Coater Operator
Coating Operator
Cold Head Operator
Cold Mill Operator
Cold Milling Machine Operator
Compacting Machine Operator
Compacting Machine Setter
Compacting Machine Tender
Compound Specialist
Compressor Operator
Compressor Station Operator
Computer Numerical Control (CNC) Lathe Machine Operator
Computer Numerical Control (CNC) Lathe Operator
Computer Numerical Control (CNC) Machine Operator
Computer Numerical Control (CNC) Machinist
Computer Numerical Control (CNC) Mill Operator
Computer Numerical Control (CNC) Milling Machine Operator
Computer Numerical Control (CNC) Operator
Computer Numerical Control (CNC) Set-Up Operator
Computer Numerical Control (CNC) Set-Up Technician
Computer-Controlled Machine Tool Operator
Computer-Controlled Robot Tool Operator
Continuous Operator
Control Area Manager
Control Area Operator
Control Center Manager
Control Center Operator
Control Manager
Control Operator

Manufacturing Production & Operations

Control Room Equipment Operator
Control Room Manager
Control Room Operator
Control Room Supervisor
Core Machine Operator
Core Making Operator
Crane Man
Crane Operator
Crown & Bridge Dental Laboratory (Lab) Technician
Crozer Machine Operator
Crude Oil Pump System Operator
Crusher Operator
Crushing Machine Operator
Cutter Operator
Delimber Operator
Dental Ceramist
Dental Laboratory (Lab) Bench Worker
Dental Laboratory (Lab) Technician
Denture Technician
Die Setter
Digital Photography Operator
Digital Printer Operator
Direct Casting Operator
Director of Manufacturing
Director of Operations
Director of Production
Director of Production Operations
Distribution Manager
Distribution Operations
Distribution Operations Manager
Distribution Operations Supervisor
Distribution Systems Manager
Distribution Systems Supervisor
Dragline Operator
Dredge Operator
Drier Operator
Dry Kiln Operator
Edger Technician
Electric Melt Operator

Electric Motor Compressor Operator
Electric System Operator
Electrical Equipment Assembler
Electrical Equipment Installer
Electrical Equipment Technician
Electrical Parts Assembler
Electrical Parts Installer
Electrical Technician
Electromechanical Assembler
Electromechanical Equipment Assembler
Electromechanical Equipment Installer
Electromechanical Equipment Technician
Electromechanical Parts Assembler
Electromechanical Parts Installer
Electromechanical Technician
Electronic Assembler
Electronic Equipment Assembler
Electronic Equipment Installer
Electronic Parts Assembler
Electronic Parts Installer
Electronic Prepress (EPP) Operator
Electronic Prepress (EPP) Technician
Electronics Equipment Technician
Electronics Technician
End Loader Operator
Engine Assembler
Engine Builder
Engine Installer
Engine Room Operator
Engine Technician
Engineering Manager
Equipment & Machine Operators
Equipment Auditor
Equipment Inspector
Equipment Manager
Equipment Operator
Equipment Technician
Excavating Equipment Operator
Extruder Operator

Manufacturing Production & Operations

Extruding Machine Operator
Extruding Machine Setter
Extruding Machine Tender
Extrusion Operator
Fabricator
Facilities Manager
Factory Assembler
Factory Worker
Farm Equipment Operator
Farm Machinery Operator
Farm Manager
Feller Buncher Operator
Fiberglass Finisher
Field Operator
Film Processor
Finisher
Finishing Laboratory (Lab) Technician
Flattening Machine Operator
Flowpath Manager
Forge Operator
Forge Press Operator
Forging Machine Operator
Forklift Operator
Forming Machine Operator
Forming Machine Setter
Forming Machine Tender
Foundry Mold Operator
Foundry Operator
Front End Loader Operator
Fuel Injection Technician
Furnace Operator
Fuselage Assembler
Gas Compressor Operator
Gas Controller
Gas Dispatcher
Gas Plant Operator
Gas System Operator
Gas Terminal Operator
General Manager

Grapple Skidder Operator
Grinder Operator
Grinding Machine Operator
Head Operator
Head Sawyer
Header Set-Up Operator
Hearing Aid Technician
Heat Treat Operator
Heat Treat Technician
Heating Systems Assembler
Heating Systems Installer
Heavy Equipment Operator
Helicopter Assembler
Helicopter Engine Assembler
Helicopter Engine Builder
Helicopter Engine Installer
Helicopter Engine Technician
Helicopter Structural Assembler
Helicopter Systems Assembler
Helicopter Systems Installation
Helicopter Systems Installer
High-Frequency Mill Operator
High-Frequency Milling Machine Operator
High-Speed Pressman
Horticultural Manager
Hydraulic Tractor Operator
Industrial Machinist
Industrial Manager
Industrial Painter
Industrial Plant Manager
Industrial Production Manager
Inspector
Internal Combustion Compressor Operator
Inventory Analyst
Inventory Control Analyst
Inventory Control Manager
Inventory Manager
Issuing Operator
Jet Engine Assembler

Manufacturing Production & Operations

Jet Engine Builder
Jet Engine Installer
Jet Engine Technician
Kettle Operator
Kiln Fireman
Kiln Operator
Knot Saw Operator
Knot Sawyer
Laboratory Technician
Landing Gear Assembler
Landing Gear Installer
Lapping Machine Operator
Lathe Operator
Licensed Orthotist Assistant
Liquefied Natural Gas (LNG) Plant Operator
Liquefied Natural Gas (LNG) Specialist
Liquefied Natural Gas (LNG) Technician
Loader Operator
Loading Machine Operator
Locomotive Engine Assembler
Locomotive Engine Builder
Locomotive Engine Installer
Locomotive Engine Technician
Log Processor Operator
Logging Equipment Operator
Logging Shovel Operator
Machine Operator
Machine Setter
Machine Tender
Machinist
Maintenance Machinist
Maintenance Manager
Manufacturing Associate
Manufacturing Engineer
Manufacturing Engineering Manager
Manufacturing Manager
Manufacturing Operations Manager
Manufacturing Supervisor
Materials Auditor

Materials Inspector
Materials Manager
Melt Room Operator
Melt Supervisor
Metal Finisher
Metal Model Maker
Metal-Refining Furnace Operator
Microwave Extruder Operator
Mill Operator
Mill Room Operator
Milling Machine Operator
Mining Equipment Operator
Missile Assembler
Mixing Machine Operator
Mobile Crane Operator
Model & Die Worker
Model Maker
Mold Maker
Mold Tooling Designer (MTD)
Molding Operator
Molding Technician
Multi-Blade Sawyer
Multi-Skill Operator
Natural Gas Terminal Operator
Nuclear Control Operator
Nuclear Control Room Non-Licensed Operator
Nuclear Control Room Operator
Nuclear Control Room Supervisor
Nuclear Operator
Nuclear Plant Operator (NPO)
Nuclear Power Reactor Operator
Nuclear Station Operator
Numerical Control (CNC) Lathe Machine Operator
Numerical Control (CNC) Lathe Operator
Numerical Control (CNC) Machine Operator
Numerical Control (CNC) Machinist
Numerical Control (CNC) Mill Operator
Numerical Control (CNC) Milling Machine Operator
Numerical Control (CNC) Operator

Manufacturing Production & Operations

Numerical Control (CNC) Planing Machine Operator
Numerical Control (CNC) Set-Up Operator
Numerical Control (CNC) Set-Up Technician
Numerical Control Programmer
Offset Pressman
Oil Pump System Operator
Operating Engineer
Operations & Maintenance (O&M) Technician
Operations Manager
Operations Superintendent
Operations Supervisor
Operations Technician
Operator
Optical Laboratory (Lab) Technician
Optical Technician
Orthopedic Technician
Orthotic & Prosthetic (O&P) Technician
Orthotic Technician
Orthotics Laboratory (Lab) Technician
Outside Operator
Oven Operator
Overhead Crane Operator
Painter
Parts Assembler
Parts Inspector
Parts Installer
Patternmaker
Permanent Fixtures
Petroleum Plant Operator
Petroleum Pump System Operator
Photographic Laboratory (Lab) Manager
Photographic Laboratory (Lab) Technician
Photographic Processing Equipment Operator
Photographic Processing Machine Operator
Photographic Specialist
Photographic Technician
Pilot Plant Manager
Pipefitter
Pipeline Systems Operator

Pipeline Technician
Pit Operator
Plant Control Manager
Plant Control Operator
Plant Engineer
Plant Engineering Manager
Plant Manager
Plant Operating Engineer
Plant Operations Manager
Plant Operator
Plant Superintendent
Plant Supervisor
Plant Utilities Engineer
Plate Maker
Polishing Machine Operator
Porcelain Technician
Port Crane Operator
Power Plant Manager
Power Plant Operator
Power Plant Supervisor
Power Systems Dispatcher
Power Systems Manager
Power Systems Operator
Power Systems Supervisor
Precision Machinist
Prefabricated Parts Assembler
Prefabricated Parts Inspector
Prefabricated Parts Installer
Prepress Operator
Prepress Stripper
Prepress Technician
Press Operator
Pressing Machine Operator
Pressing Machine Setter
Pressing Machine Tender
Pressman
Printed Circuit Board (PCB) Tester
Printing Press Operator
Printing Pressman

Manufacturing Production & Operations

Process Control Programmer
Process Development Technician
Process Manager
Process Operator
Process Technician
Product Auditor
Product Engineer
Product Inspector
Product Line Manager
Product Line Supervisor
Product Manager
Production Control Manager
Production Machinist
Production Manager
Production Operations Manager
Production Operator
Production Planner
Production Supervisor
Production Technician
Production Worker
Project Manager
Prosthetics Laboratory (Lab) Technician
Prosthetics Technician
Quality Assurance Analyst
Quality Assurance Auditor
Quality Assurance Inspector
Quality Assurance Manager
Quality Assurance Supervisor
Quality Assurance Technician
Quality Auditor
Quality Control Auditor
Quality Control Inspector
Quality Control Manager
Quality Control Supervisor
Quality Control Technician
Quality Inspector
Quality Manager
Quality Supervisor
Quality Technician

Radio Control Crane Operator
Reactor Operator (RO)
Refinery Operator
Registered Orthotic Technician (ROT)
Registered Prosthetic Technician (RPT)
Registered Prosthetic-Orthotic Technician (RPOT)
Repair Manager
Rip Saw Operator
Roll Form Operator
Rolling Machine Operator
Roughing Mill Operator
Rubber Extrusion Operator
Sample Maker
Saw Operator
Sawing Machine Operator
Sawing Operator
Sawyer
Scarf & Anneal Operator
Scrap Crane Operator
Screw Machine Operator
Scroll Saw Operator
Set-Up Machinist
Shear Operator
Sheet Metal Assembler & Riveter (SMAR)
Sheet Metal Fabricator
Shell Core Operator
Shell Mold Operator
Shift Supervisor
Ship Engine Assembler
Ship Engine Builder
Ship Engine Installer
Ship Engine Technician
Silk Screen Operator
Skidder Driver
Skidder Operator
Slurry Control Operator
Spray Dry Operator
Spray Painter
Stationary Engineer

Manufacturing Production & Operations

Stationary Steam Engineer
Stationery Engineer
Steam Compressor Operator
Stock Preparation Operator
Storage Manager
Structural Assembler
Structures Installer
Structures Technician
Superintendent
Surfacing Technician
System Operator
Tail Assembler
Tail Installer
Tempering Machine Operator
Terminal Operator
Thinning Machine Operator
Tool & Die Maker
Tool Designer
Tool Maker
Track Hoe Operator
Tractor Operator
Transmission Systems Operator
Tuber Operator
Ultrasonic Equipment Operator
Underground Loading Machine Operator
Unit Operator
Unit Reactor Operator
Upkeep Mechanic
Utility Operator
Utility Person
Ventilating Systems Assembler
Vertical Computer Numerical Control (CNC) Operator
Vessel Operator
Vice President of Distribution
Vice President of Manufacturing
Vice President of Operations
Vice President of Production
Visual Inspector
Welder

Wing Assembler
Wing Installer
Wiring Installer
Wiring Technician
Woodyard Crane Operator

Manufacturing Production & Operations

Software, Systems & Technology

1CadCam Unigraphics
24/7 Systems Software Solutions
3rd Dimension Systems Software
Adobe Acrobat
Aldata G.O.L.D.
Anix Software HTML-View
Anix Software MyThumbnails
Anix Software PicViewer
Argos Software ABECAS Insight WMS
ATMS StockTrack PLUS
Citect IIM
CitectSCADA
Clockware
Computer-Aided Design & Drafting (CADD) Software
Computer-Aided Design (CAD) Software
Computer-Aided Manufacturing (CAM) Software
Computer-Integrated Manufacturing (CIM) Time Manager
Computer-Integrated Manufacturing (CIM) Warehouse Shipping Manager
CorVu
DataModes TM/4
Diversicon Technologies VisuTrac
Edit CNC Software
Enterprise Resource Planning (ERP) Software
FileMaker Pro
Full Capacity International Software Suite
GSupply Solutions ShopTrakker
IBM Lotus 1-2-3
IBM Lotus Notes
IBM Rationale ClearQuest
INMASS
Integrated Materials Management System
Intuit QuickBooks
Kentch Trig Kalculator
Kentech Kipware PLN
Kronos Workforce Timekeeper

Lighthammer Software
Logistics Management Software
M&D Systems Myte Myke Software
MAGI
MAPICS
Materials Management Software
Materials Requirements Planning (MRP)
MESA International Software
Micro Computer Systems TMInvent Software
Microsoft Access
Microsoft Excel
Microsoft Outlook
Microsoft PowerPoint
Microsoft Project
Microsoft Total Quality Control Management
Microsoft Windows
Microsoft Word
MSI Software Solutions
Parable Software Suite
Peartree ERP Software
ProfitKey International Software Suite
Project Management Software
Proleit AG Software Suite
QA Software QMS Materials Management
RedPrairie DLx Warehouse
Retain Resource Planning
RGM Software
Sac River Systems HyperTools
Sac River Systems PowerTools
Sac River Systems ProBase
SAP Business One
SAP Inventory
SAP Warehouse Management
SoftSelect Systems Software Suite
Solid State Software Solutions
SolidWorks CAD
SSA Global Supply Chain Management
Supply Chain Software
SY-CON PC-Toolcrib Inventory Management Software

Manufacturing Production & Operations

Tamlin Software Manufacturing Conductor
Technology Group International Enterprise 21 ERP
Time Accounting Software
Timekeeping Software
TISCOR Software Suite
Tool-TracK
Total Quality Management (TQM) Software
Tuttle Sullivan
UGS Solid Edge
Vanguard Business Analytics Software
Vero International VISI-Series
Wonderware DT Analyst Plant Productivity Improvement
Work Technology WorkTech Time

Principal Manufacturing & Production Industries

Aerospace
Agriculture
Aircraft
Apparel
Automotive
Boat
Coal
Chemical
Computer
Clay
Computer
Concrete
Dental
Electrical
Electronics
Food
Furniture
Garment
Gas
Glass
Leather
Lumber
Machinery
Marine
Medical
Metals
Minerals
Oil
Petroleum
Pharmaceutical
Plastic
Pulp & Paper
Rubber
Ship
Stone

Manufacturing Production & Operations

Textile
Toy
Vehicle
Wood

KeyWords & KeyWord Phrases for Manufacturing & Production Operations

0-1 Drop Indicator
Accelerometer
Adjustable Wrench
Agriculture
Air Hose
Algebra
Alignment
Alligator Jaw Compression Riveter
Animal Husbandry
Apprenticeship
Aquaculture
Arc Welding
Arc Welding Equipment
Area Plant Management
Area Plant Operations
Area Plant Operations Management
Area Production Management
Area Production Operations
Area Production Operations Management
Arithmetic
Assembly
Assembly Line Management
Assembly Management
Asset Management
Attachments
Automated Control Systems
Automated Controls
Automated Manufacturing
Automated Parts Loading
Automatic Feeding Device
Automatic Feeding Mechanism
Automatic Measuring Equipment
Automatic Tool Change
Automation
Backplate Tester

Backup Wrench
Beading Tool
Bench Grinder
Bending
Blow Molding
Blueprint
Blueprint Lines
Bolts
Bore Gauge
Brazing
Brazing Equipment
Bubble Leak Analyzer
Calculus
Calibrated Resistance Measuring Equipment
Caliper
Calorimetric Leak Tester
Capacitive Acceleration Instrument
Capacity
Capacity Planning
Capital
Capital Asset
Capital Budget
Capital Project
Capital Project Management
Capital Resources
Cell Manufacturing
Chips
Circuit Board
Circuits
Clamps
Commodities
Computer Applications
Computer Controls
Computer Engineering
Computer Hardware
Computer Integrated Manufacturing (CIM)
Computer Numerically Controlled (CNC) Machine
Computer Programming
Computer Software

Computer Technology
Computer-Aided Design & Drafting (CADD)
Computer-Aided Design (CAD)
Computer-Aided Manufacturing (CAM)
Computer-Integrated Manufacturing (CIM)
Computerized Controls
Concurrent Engineering
Continuous Improvement
Continuous Operations
Continuous Process Improvement
Continuous Quality Improvement
Control Board
Control Instruments
Coolant
Coolant Flow
Cost Avoidance
Cost Elimination
Cost Management
Cost Reduction
Costs
Crane
Crimping
Crimping Tool
Cross-Functional Team
Cutting
Cutting Equipment
Cutting Tool
Cycle Time
Cycle Time Reduction
Data
Data Analysis
Data Collection
Defect
Defect Analysis
Defect Reporting
Design
Dial Caliper
Dial Indicator
Dials

Manufacturing Production & Operations

Digital Resistance Meter
Dimensions
Distribution
Distribution Management
Distribution Operations
Distribution Operations Management
Dolly
Drafting
Drafting Template
Drawings
Efficiency
Efficiency Improvement
Electrical Assembly
Electrical Discharge Machine (EDM)
Electrical Engineering
Electricity
Electromechanical Assembly
Electromechanical Engineering
Electronic Equipment
Electronics
Electronics Assembly
Electronics Engineering
Engineering
Engineering Management
Engineering Science
Engineering Technology
Environment
Environmental Health & Safety (EHS)
Environmental Impact
Equipment
Equipment Financing
Equipment Maintenance
Equipment Operations
Equipment Repair
Ergonomically Efficient
Ergonomics
Expense Control
Expense Management
Expenses

Export
Exportation
Extruding Machine
Extrusion
Fabricate
Fabrication
Facilities
Facilities Consolidation
Facilities Construction
Facilities Management
Facilities Renovation
Factory
Factory Assembly
Fasteners
Filament
Filing
Finished Goods
Finished Products
Fixtures
Flaring Tool
Flowmeter
Flowpath
Flowpath Management
Food & Drug Administration (FDA)
Forklift
Forklift Operations
Forming
Forming Machine
Front-End Loader
Fuel Control Wrench
Functional Gauge
Gas Welding
Gas Welding Equipment
Gauges
Gears
Geometry
Grinder
Grinding Machine
Guide Jig

Manufacturing Production & Operations

Hammer Drill
Hand Drill
Hand File
Hand Ramming Tool
Hand Tools
Hand Truck
Handwheels
Hazardous Materials (HAZMAT)
Hoist
Hopper
Horticulture
Hydraulic Lift
Hydraulic System
Hydraulics
Illustrations
Import
Importation
In-Circuit Tester
Index Points
Industrial
Industrial Engineering
Industrial Machinery
Industrial Management
Industrial Operations
Industrial Plant
Industrial Production
Industrial Technology
Industry
Inspection
Inspection Fixture
Installation
Instrument Readings
Instrumentation
Instruments
Integrated Circuit Testers
Integrated Logistics Management (ILM)
Integrated Logistics Support (ILS)
International Organization for Standardization (ISO 9000 / ISO 14000)
Inventory

Inventory Control
Inventory Management
Inventory Planning
Jig
Just-In-Time (JIT)
Just-In-Time (JIT) Manufacturing
Kaizen
Labor
Labor Efficiency
Labor Relations
Lapping Tools
Lathe
Layout
Layout Tools
Leak
Leak Testing
Leak Testing Equipment
Lean Manufacturing
Line Reamers
Logistics
Machine
Machine Chuck
Machine Feed
Machine Feed Ratios
Machine Gauges
Machine Operations
Machine Shop
Machine Speed
Machine Spindle
Machine Table
Magnetic Induction Acceleration Instrument
Maintenance
Maintenance Management
Manufacturing Cell
Manufacturing Engineering
Manufacturing Engineering Management
Manufacturing Integration
Manufacturing Management
Manufacturing Operations

Manufacturing Production & Operations

Manufacturing Operations Management
Manufacturing Technology
Marking Instrument
Mass Flow Leak Tester
Master Schedule
Material Guiding Jig
Material Hoisting Sling
Materials
Materials Assembly
Materials Planning
Materials Science
Mathematics
Measurements
Measuring
Measuring Instruments
Mechanical
Mechanical Assembly
Mechanical Drawing
Mechanical Engineering
Mechanical Instruments
Metal
Metal Bending
Metal Bending Equipment
Metal Bucking Bar
Meter
Meter Readings
Micro-Welding
Micro-Welding Equipment
Micro-Welding Machine
Mini Loader
Mixer
Mixing
Motion
Multi-Site Operations
Multi-Skill Operations
Mylar Index Template
National Institute of Metalworking Skills (NIMS)
National Tooling & Machining Association (NTMA)
Numerical Tool & Process Control

Occupational Health
Occupational Health & Safety (OH&S)
Occupational Health & Safety Administration (OSHA)
Occupational Safety
Offshore
Offshore Assembly
Offshore Manufacturing
Oil
On-Time Delivery
Operating Budget
Operations
Operations & Maintenance (O&M)
Operations Control
Operations Management
Operations Monitoring
Operations Reengineering
Operations Start-Up
Operations Technology
Optical Gauge
Optimization
Order
Order Fulfillment
Order Processing
Organic
Outside Operations
Outsourcing
Overhead Crane
Pallet
Pallet Mover
Pallet Truck
Panel
Panel Board
Panel Lights
Participative Management
Parts
Parts Assembly
Parts Inspection
Parts Installation
Performance Analysis

Manufacturing Production & Operations

Performance Improvement
Performance Measurement
Performance Metrics
Physical Inventory
Physics
Piezoelectric Acceleration Instrument
Pilot Manufacturing
Pilot Plant
Pin Gauge
Plant Engineering
Plant Engineering Management
Plant Management
Plant Operations
Plant Operations Management
Plug Gauge
Pneumatic Ramming Tool
Pneumatic System
Pneumatics
Policies & Procedures
Polisher
Polymer
Power Tools
Precision
Precision
Precision Machine
Precision Machine Products Association (PMPA)
Precision Measurement
Precision Measurements
Precision Measuring Instrument
Precision Tapered Reamer
Precision Template
Precision Tools
Prefabricated Parts
Prefabricated Parts Assembly
Prefabricated Parts Inspection
Prefabricated Parts Installation
Pressure
Printed Circuit Board (PCB)
Process

Process Automation
Process Development
Process Redesign
Process Reengineering
Process Technology
Processing
Processing Time
Processor
Procurement
Product Assembly
Product Development
Product Engineering
Product Management
Product Quality
Product Rationalization
Product Research & Development (R&D)
Product Specifications
Product Standards
Production
Production Expediting
Production Forecasting
Production Lead Time
Production Management
Production Methods
Production Operations
Production Operations Management
Production Planning
Production Processes
Production Scheduling
Production Specifications
Production Yield
Productivity
Productivity Improvement
Profit & Loss (P&L)
Profit & Loss (P&L) Management
Programmable Logic Controller (PLC)
Programmable Motion Control Device
Project Budget
Purchasing

Manufacturing Production & Operations

Purchasing Management
Quality
Quality Assurance
Quality Circle
Quality Control
Quality Control Test
Quality Improvement
Quality Standards
Ramming Tool
Ranch Management
Raw Materials
Raw Products
Reamer
Receiving
Recoilless Rivet Hammer
Recording Instruments
Recordkeeping
Regulations
Regulatory
Regulatory Affairs
Regulatory Compliance
Regulatory Reporting
Repair
Repair Management
Replacement
Replacement Assembly
Replacement Parts
Reporting
Research & Development (R&D)
Resistance Meter
Resistivity Meter
Resonance Acceleration Instrument
Resource Management
Resources
Ring Filling Wheel
Rivet
Rivet Gun
Rivet Tools
Robot

Robotics
Safety
Safety Equipment
Safety Management
Safety Training
Scale
Scheduling
Schematics
Scraper
Screw
Semi-Automatic Equipment
Semiconductor
Semi-Finished Goods
Setup Template
Sheet Metal
Sheet Metal Assembly
Sheet Metal Fabrication
Shipping
Shipping & Receiving
Shipping & Receiving Operation
Six Sigma
Sling
Smoothing
Soldering
Soldering Equipment
Soldering Gun
Soldering Machine
Solvent
Spare Parts
Spares & Repairs Management
Specifications
Statistical Analysis
Statistical Process Control (SPC)
Statistics
Storage
Structural Assembly
Structural Engineering
Subassembly
Supply Chain

Manufacturing Production & Operations

Supply Chain Management
Surface Grinder
Switches
Synchronizing Cam
Tank
Tap
Team Building
Team Leadership
Technical Drawings
Technical Illustrations
Technical Instructions
Technical Manual
Technology
Technology Integration
Technology Operation
Technology Optimization
Temperature
Temperature Regulation
Template
Tender
Test
Test Results
Testing
Time
Time & Motion Studies
Tolerance
Tool & Die
Tool-Holding Device
Torque
Torque Driver
Torque Wrench
Total Quality Management (TQM)
Traffic Management
Training & Development
Trimming
Troubleshooting
Trunnion Centering Tool
Trunnion Wrench
Tube

Tube Bending
Tube Bending Machinery
Tube End Finisher
Tumbler
Turnaround Management
Union Negotiations
Union Relations
Union-Management Negotiations
Union-Management Relations
Utilities
Utilities Management
Utility Operations
Vacuum
Value-Added Process
Valves
Vendor
Vendor Management
Vendor Selection
Vendor Sourcing
Vernier Caliper
Vibration
Vibration
Vibration Control
Visual Inspection
Vocational School
Vocational Training
Warehousing Operations
Weighing
Weight
Weight & Measurement
Welding
Welding Equipment
Welding Machine
Wheel Loader
Wiring
Work in Progress (WIP)
Work Order
Workflow
Workflow Optimization

Workflow Scheduling
Workforce
Workforce Management
Workpieces
Workshop Crane
World Class Manufacturing (WCM)
Yield
Yield Improvement
Yield Management

Additional KeyWords & KeyWord Phrases for Aircraft Structure, Surface, Rigging & Systems Assembly

Aircraft
Aircraft Assembly
Aircraft Line
Aircraft Line Assembly
Aircraft Rigging
Aircraft Structural Assembly
Aircraft Structures
Aircraft Surfaces
Aircraft Systems
Aircraft Systems Assembly
Aircraft Systems Installation
Airframe
Airframe Assembly
Airframe Structural Assembly
Airframe Structure Installation
Airframe Systems
Airframe Systems Assembly
Airframe Systems Installation
Airplane
Airplane Assembly
Airplane Line
Airplane Line Assembly
Airplane Rigging
Airplane Structural Assembly
Airplane Structures
Airplane Systems
Airplane Systems Assembly
Airplane Systems Installation
Aviation Structures
Aviation Surfaces
Aviation Systems
Aviation Systems Assembly
Aviation Systems Installation
Avionics

Manufacturing Production & Operations

Bulkhead
Bulkhead Assembly
Bulkhead Installation
Composite Materials
Composites
Federal Aviation Administration (FAA)
Fittings
Fuselage
Fuselage Assembly
Fuselage Installation
Heating Systems
Heating Systems Assembly
Heating Systems Installation
Helicopter
Helicopter Assembly
Helicopter Structural Assembly
Helicopter Systems
Helicopter Systems Assembly
Helicopter Systems Installation
Landing Gear
Landing Gear Assembly
Landing Gear Installation
Missile
Missile Assembly
Propeller-Driven Aircraft
Rigging
Rigging & Control Equipment
Space Vehicle
Stabilizer
Structural Assembly
Structures Installation
Tail Assembly
Tail Installation
Tails
Ventilating Systems
Ventilating Systems Assembly
Wing Assembly
Wing Installation
Wings

Additional KeyWords & KeyWord Phrases for Chemical Plant Operations

Air
Air Flow
Air Flow Monitoring
Air Flow Regulations
Blending
Blending Vessel
Chemical Change
Chemical Characteristics
Chemical Composition
Chemical Disposal
Chemical Gases
Chemical Ingredients
Chemical Interactions
Chemical Leaks
Chemical Liquids
Chemical Operations
Chemical Plant
Chemical Plant Operations
Chemical Plant Operations Technology
Chemical Processing
Chemical Production Techniques
Chemical Properties
Chemical Quality
Chemical Reactions
Chemical Structures
Chemical Transformations
Chemical Yields
Chemicals
Chemistry
Chlorination
Chlorination
Chlorination Operation
Chlorine
Control Room
Control Room Operations
Converter

Manufacturing Production & Operations

Converter Vessel
Devulcanizer
Exhaust
Exhaust Fumes
Exhaust Gases
Feed
Feed Regulation
Flow
Flow Regulation
Gravity
Oil
Oil Flow
Oil Flow Monitoring
Oil Flow Regulation
pH
pH Level
Prescribed Reactions
Pressure
Pressure Regulation
Reactor
Reactor Vessel
Spray Dry Operation
Steam
Steam Flow
Steam Flow Monitoring
Steam Flow Regulation
Steam-Jacketed Kettles
Substances
Trough
Vessel Operation
Viscosity

Additional KeyWords & KeyWord Phrases for Coating, Painting, Plating & Spraying Machine Operations

Air Bubble
Anodizer
Anodizing Line Operations
Automated Paint Mixing Equipment
Chrome
Chrome Plating
Cleaning Solution
Coating
Coating Equipment
Coating Machinery
Coating Operations
Coating Quality
Conductive Solution
Copper
Coverage
Electroplate
Enamel
Glaze
Hand Sprayer
Hard Chrome Plater
Hard Chrome Plating
Lacquer
Liquid Metal
Liquid Metal Solution
Liquid Plastic
Liquid Plastic Solution
Machine-Fed Carriage
Machine-Fed Spindle
Paint
Paint Flow
Paint Viscosity
Painting
Painting Equipment
Painting Machinery

Manufacturing Production & Operations

Painting Operations
Plating
Plating Operations
Powder
Powder Coater
Press
Press Operations
Rubber
Rust
Rust Proofing
Silk Screen
Silk Screen Operations
Silver
Spray Painting
Sprayer
Spraying
Spraying Equipment
Spraying Machinery
Spraying Operations
Uneven Coverage
Varnish
Viscometer
Viscosity

Additional KeyWords & KeyWord Phrases for Crane & Tower Operations

Block Devices
Blocking
Boom
Cable
Cherry Picker
Clamps
Clips
Crane
Crane Attachment
Crane Mechanism
Electromagnetic
Floor Scale
Friction Crane
Gantry Crane
Grappling Device
Lifting
Lifting Accessories
Lifting Capacity
Lifting Magnet
Load Weight
Luffing Jib Crane
Machine Movement
Materials Movement
Mechanical Boom
Moving
Outrigging
Overhead Crane
Placement
Pulley
Ringer Crane
Scale
Shackles
Spreader
Tower
Tower Attachment

Manufacturing Production & Operations

Tower Equipment
Tower Technology
Wedge Socket
Weight
Woodyard Crane

Additional KeyWords & KeyWord Phrases for Crushing, Grinding & Polishing Machine Operations

Batch
Batch Mixer
Batch Mixing
Beveller
Beveller Operations
Blending
Blending Machine
Blending Machine Operations
Blending Operations
Buffing
Buffing Machine Operations
Chipping Hammer
Coal
Crushing
Crushing Machine
Crushing Machine Operations
Crushing Operations
Cullet Trucker
Debar
Deburring
Fiberglass Finisheing
Food
Glass
Grain
Grind
Grind Fineness
Grinder
Grinding
Grinding Machine
Grinding Machine Operations
Grinding Operations
Hone
Lap
Lapping
Lapping Machine Operations

Manufacturing Production & Operations

Mill Operations
Milling
Polish
Polishing Machine
Polishing Machine Operations
Polishing Operations
Rubber
Shear
Slurry
Slurry Control Operations
Stone

Additional KeyWords & KeyWord Phrases for Dredging, Excavating & Loading Equipment Operations

Anchor
Auger
Backfill
Backfilling
Boom Conveyor
Cable-Drawn Scoop
Cable-Drawn Scrapper
Cables
Coal
Compact Excavator
Concrete
Conveyor Boom
Crawler-Mounted Draglines
Cutterhead
Depth
Depth Finding
Depth Gauges
Depth Measurements
Digging Plan
Dragline
Dredge
Dredge Operations
Dredging
Excavate
Excavated Material
Excavating Equipment
Excavating Machinery
Excavating Technology
Excavation
Front End Loader
Gathering Arm
Gathering-Arm Motor
Grade Stake
Gravel

Manufacturing Production & Operations

Hopper
Hopper Car
Hydraulic Excavator
Hydraulic Pump
Lake
Loading Machine
Mine
Mine Car
Mine Contents
Mini Excavator
Mining
Mining Equipment
Mining Machinery
Mobile Excavator
Navigable Waterway
Open-Top Box Car
Open-Top Rail Car
Ore
Pipe
Pipe Laying
Pontoon
Pontoon Boat
Power Auger
Pump
River
Rocks
Sand
Shore Anchor
Shore Cable
Shuttle Car
Side-Drop Car
Spillage
Stones
Stream
Suction
Suction Boom
Telescoping Excavator
Tracked Excavator
Underground Loading Machine

Water Pump

Additional KeyWords & KeyWord Phrases for Electrical & Electronic Equipment Assembly

Actuator
Armature
Armature Assembly
Armature Installation
Breaker
Breaker Unit
Breaker Unit Assembly
Breaker Unit Installation
Control Linkage
Dynamometer
Electrical
Electrical Equipment
Electrical Equipment Assembly
Electrical Equipment Installation
Electrical Parts
Electrical Parts Assembly
Electrical Parts Installation
Electromechanical
Electromechanical Assembly
Electromechanical Equipment
Electromechanical Equipment Assembly
Electromechanical Equipment Installation
Electromechanical Parts
Electromechanical Parts Assembly
Electromechanical Parts Installation
Electronic Assembly
Electronic Equipment
Electronic Equipment Assembly
Electronic Equipment Installation
Electronic Parts
Electronic Parts Assembly
Electronic Parts Installation
Electronics
Electronics Technology
Gyros

Gyroscope
Magnetic Drum
Resistance
Resistance Factors
Servomechanism
Wire
Wiring
Wiring Assembly
Wiring Circuits
Wiring Diagram
Wiring Installation

Manufacturing Production & Operations

Additional KeyWords & KeyWord Phrases for Engine & Other Machines Assembly

Aircraft Engine
Aircraft Engine Assembly
Aircraft Engine Building
Aircraft Engine Installation
Aircraft Engine Technology
Airplane Engine
Airplane Engine Assembly
Airplane Engine Building
Airplane Engine Installation
Airplane Engine Technology
Automotive Engine
Automotive Engine Assembly
Automotive Engine Building
Automotive Engine Installation
Automotive Engine Technology
Engine
Engine Assembly
Engine Installation
Engine Technology
Helicopter Engine
Helicopter Engine Assembly
Helicopter Engine Building
Helicopter Engine Installation
Helicopter Engine Technology
Jet Engine
Jet Engine Assembly
Jet Engine Installation
Jet Engine Technology
Locomotive Engine
Locomotive Engine Assembly
Locomotive Engine Building
Locomotive Engine Installation
Locomotive Engine Technology
Ship Engine
Ship Engine Assembly

Ship Engine Building
Ship Engine Installation
Ship Engine Technology

Manufacturing Production & Operations

Additional KeyWords & KeyWord Phrases for Extruding, Forming, Pressing & Compacting Machine Operations

Brick
Compacting
Compacting Machine Operations
Compacting Machine Setting
Cosmetics
Extruding
Extruding Machine Operations
Extruding Machine Setting
Extrusion
Extrusion Operation
Food
Forming
Forming Machine Operations
Forming Machine Setting
Glass-Forming Machine
Glassware
Job Change Crew
Microwave Extruder Operations
Mill Room Machine Operations
Plodder Machine
Pressing
Pressing Machine Operations
Pressing Machine Setting
Rubber
Rubber Extrusion
Rubber Extrusion Operations
Soap
Tile
Tobacco
Tuber Machine
Tuber Operations
Wax

Additional KeyWords & KeyWord Phrases for Farming & Agricultural Machine & Equipment Operations

Agricultural Equipment
Agricultural Machinery
American Society of Farm Managers & Rural Appraisers (ASFMRA)
Bale
Baler
Conveyor
Crop Baling
Crop Cultivation
Crop Farming
Crop Harvesting
Crop Management
Crop Management
Crop Rotation
Crop Storage
Crops
Cultivation
Discs
Farm Equipment
Farm Machinery
Farm Management
Fertilizer
Forklift
Fungus
Ginning
Harvest
Harvesting
Hay
Hay Bucking
Hopper
Husking
Insecticides
Insects
Irrigation
Land

Manufacturing Production & Operations

Land Cultivation
Land Management
Livestock
Livestock Farming
Organic
Organic Farming
Organic Foods
Pesticides
Planter
Planter Machinery
Planting
Plants
Plow
Shelling
Soil
Soil Irrigation
Sprayer
Sprayer Machinery
Suction Gate
Threshing
Tilling
Tractor
Transfer Auger
Weed Control
Weeding
Weeds

Additional KeyWords & KeyWord Phrases for Forging Machine & Foundry Operations

Bending
Cold Forging
Cold Head Operations
Core
Core Box
Core Machine Operations
Core Machinery
Core Maker
Core Making
Core Making Operations
Core Stripper
Core Stripping
Cutting
Die
Die Casting
Die Mold
Die Molding
Flattening
Forge Operations
Forge Press
Forge Press Equipment
Forge Press Machinery
Forge Press Operations
Forging
Forging Equipment
Forging Machine
Forging Machine Equipment
Forging Machine Operations
Forming
Foundry
Foundry Equipment
Foundry Machinery
Foundry Mold
Foundry Mold Operations
Foundry Operations

Manufacturing Production & Operations

Hammer Operations
Header Set-Up Operations
Hot Forging
Machined Part
Manipulator Operations
Metal
Metal Casting
Metal Forming
Mold
Mold Assembly
Mold Pouring
Mold Reassembly
Mold Reinforcement
Mold Section
Molding
Molding Equipment
Molding Machinery
Molding Operations
No-Bake Molder
No-Bake Molding
Pattern Contours
Patterns
Piercing
Pouring
Runner Holes
Sand
Sand Core
Sand Molder
Sand Molding
Shaping
Shell Core
Shell Core Equipment
Shell Core Machinery
Shell Core Operations
Shell Mold
Shell Mold Equipment
Shell Mold Machinery
Shell Mold Operations
Slab Core

Spout
Sprue Hole
Straightening
Surface
Surface Imperfections
Taper
Tapering
Wax
Wax Core

Additional KeyWords & KeyWord Phrases for Furnace, Kiln, Oven, Drier & Kettle Operations

Calciner
Calciner Operations
Drier
Drier Operations
Dry Kiln Operations
Evaporation
Evaporation Operations
Evaporator Operations
Fire
Fire Control
Fire Prevention
Fire Response
Firing
Furnace
Furnace Operations
Glass Annealing
Heating
Heating Equipment
Heating Machinery
Heating Technology
Kettle
Kettle Operations
Kiln
Kiln Operations
Lime Kiln & Recausticizing Operations
Lumber Drying
Moisture Removal
Oven
Oven Operations
Rubber Curing
Soap Boiling

Additional KeyWords & KeyWord Phrases for Gas Plant & Gas Compressor Operations

Butane
Compression
Compressor
Compressor Engine
Compressor Operations
Compressor Pumps
Compressor Station Operations
Consumption
Consumption Rate Variation
Consumption Rates
Control Room
Control Room Equipment
Control Room Equipment Operations
Dangerous Products
Electric Motor
Electric Motor Compressor
Electric Motor Compressor Operations
Engine Room
Engine Room Operations
Evaporator
Flammable
Gas
Gas Compressor
Gas Compressor Operations
Gas Dispatch
Gas Distribution
Gas Meter
Gas Meter Reader
Gas Plant
Gas Plant Operations
Gas Pressure
Gas Processing
Gas Quality
Gas Recovery
Gas System

Manufacturing Production & Operations

Gas System Operations
Gas Terminal Operations
Gas Transmission
Gases
Hydrogen
Internal Combustion
Internal Combustion Compressor
Internal Combustion Compressor Operations
Liquefied Natural Gas (LNG)
Liquefied Natural Gas (LNG) Compression
Liquefied Natural Gas (LNG) Plant Operations
Liquids
Meter
Moisture
Moisture Content
Natural Gas
Natural Gas Terminal Operations
Nitrogen
Pipeline
Pipeline Maintenance
Pipeline Repair
Pipeline Systems Operations
Powder
Powdered Materials
Power-Driven Pump
Pressure
Pressure Gauges
Pressure Regulation
Reclamation
Recovery
Refrigeration
Refrigeration Equipment
Regulator
Scrubber
Semi-Liquids
Steam
Steam Compressor
Stream Compressor Operations
Sulfur

Sulfur Content
Temperature
Terminal
Transmission
Utilities
Utility Company

Manufacturing Production & Operations

Additional KeyWords & KeyWord Phrases for Logging Equipment & Machine Operation

Board
Board Feet
Bulldozer
Bulldozer Blade
Cable Winch
Cord
Cordage
Crane
Crane Boom
Crawler
Delimb
Feller Buncher
Felling
Felling Site
Frontal Shear
Grapple
Hoisting Rack
Hydraulic Tractor
Knot Size
Knot Straightness
Limb
Log Grading
Log Landing Site
Log Loading
Log Processing
Logging
Logging Arch
Logging Equipment
Logging Equipment Operation
Logging Tractor
Sheared Trees
Shearing
Stump
Stump Pulling
Topping

Tree
Tree Clamp
Tree Harvesting
Tree Harvesting Equipment
Tree Harvesting Machinery
Tree Topping

Manufacturing Production & Operations

Additional KeyWords & KeyWord Phrases for Machine & Equipment Operation (General)

Automatic Cutting Equipment
Automatic Cutting Machinery
Automatic Loading Equipment
Automatic Loading Machinery
Automatic Packaging Equipment
Automatic Packaging Machinery
Automatic Stacking Equipment
Automatic Stacking Machinery
Auxiliary Equipment
Calibration
Clamshell Bucket
Combination Vacuum Lift
Container Reach Stacker
Container Top Handler
Conveyor Belt
Conveyors
Drop Hammer
Earth-Moving Equipment
Electric-Powered Equipment
Electric-Powered Vehicle
Elevating Platform
Equipment Calibration
Equipment Inspection
Equipment Installation
Equipment Maintenance
Equipment Malfunction
Equipment Operation
Equipment Repair
Filter
Forklift
Gas
Gasoline
Gasoline-Powered Equipment
Gasoline-Powered Vehicle
Gauges

Finding Needles in a Haystack

Gears
Grader
Hand Equipment
Hand Levels
Hand Tools
Heavy Equipment
Heavy Equipment Calibration
Heavy Equipment Inspection
Heavy Equipment Installation
Heavy Equipment Maintenance
Heavy Equipment Malfunction
Heavy Equipment Operation
Heavy Equipment Repair
Hoist
Hoisting Engine
Inclines
Industrial Control
Industrial Control System
Inspection
Instrument Readings
Instruments
Iron Ball
Laser Level
Level
Lubricate
Lubrication
Machine Control Systems
Maintenance
Maintenance & Repair
Maintenance Management
Maintenance Manual
Maintenance Operations
Man Lift
Operating Instructions
Operating Manual
Operations Specifications
Orange Peel Bucket
Overhaul Ball
Oxyacetylene Torch

Manufacturing Production & Operations

Pallet Forklift
Personnel Lift
Pile Driver
Platform Lift
Power Shovel
Power Tools
Preventive Maintenance
Propane Torch
Ramp
Repair
Repair Management
Repair Operations
Routine Maintenance
Scoop
Shovel Attachment
Skip Loader
Sliding-Boom Forklift
Straddle Carrier
Straight-Mast Forklift
Swivel Hook
Troubleshooting
Wheeled Loader
Wheeled Vehicle
Winch

Additional KeyWords & KeyWord Phrases for Machine Tool & Computer-Controlled Machine Tool Operations

5-Axis Lathe
Aluminum
Bar Stock
Bending
Bending Equipment
Bending Machine
Bore
Borer
Boring Equipment
Boring Machine
Boring Operations
Brake Press Operation
Brazing
Buffing
Buffing Equipment
Buffing Machine
CNC Mastercam
Computer Numerical Control (CNC)
Computer Numerical Control (CNC) Lathe
Computer Numerical Control (CNC) Lathe Machine Operations
Computer Numerical Control (CNC) Lathe Operations
Computer Numerical Control (CNC) Machine
Computer Numerical Control (CNC) Machine Operations
Computer Numerical Control (CNC) Machine Operations
Computer Numerical Control (CNC) Machinists' Calculator
Computer Numerical Control (CNC) Mill Operations
Computer Numerical Control (CNC) Milling Machine
Computer Numerical Control (CNC) Milling Machine Operations
Computer Numerical Control (CNC) Operations
Computer Numerical Control (CNC) Planing
Computer Numerical Control (CNC) Set Up
Computer Numerical Control (CNC) Set-Up Operations
Computer Numerical Control (CNC) Turning Center
Computer-Controlled Machine

Manufacturing Production & Operations

Computer-Controlled Machine Tool
Computer-Controlled Machine Tool Operations
Computer-Controlled Robot
Computer-Controlled Robot Tool
Computer-Controlled Robot Tool Operations
Coolant
Cooling
Cooling Mechanism
Cutting
Cutting Equipment
Cutting Machine
Die
Die Setting
Drill Press
Drilling
Drilling Equipment
Drilling Machine
Electrified Wire
Face
Facing Equipment
Facing Machine
Facing Operations
Feed Rate
Feeding
Feeding Mechanism
Finishing
Finishing Equipment
Form
Forming Equipment
Forming Machine
Forming Operations
Grinding
Grinding Equipment
Grinding Machine
Grooving
Grooving Equipment
Grooving Machine
Harmonic Vibration
Industrial Machinery

Injection Molding
Injection Molding Equipment
Injection Molding Machine
Laser
Lathe
Lathe Operations
Lubricating
Lubricating Mechanism
Lubrication
Machine Operations
Machine Speed
Maintenance Machinery
Manual Mill
Material Dimensions
Materials
Metal
Metal Work Pieces
Milling
Milling Cutter
Milling Equipment
Milling Machine
Mold
Mold Making
Mold Tooling
Mold Tooling Design
Molding
Molding Equipment
Molding Machine
Numerical Control (CNC)
Numerical Control (CNC)
Numerical Control (CNC) Lathe
Numerical Control (CNC) Lathe Machine Operations
Numerical Control (CNC) Lathe Operations
Numerical Control (CNC) Machine Operations
Numerical Control (CNC) Machinists' Calculator
Numerical Control (CNC) Mill Operations
Numerical Control (CNC) Milling Machine Operations
Numerical Control (CNC) Operations
Numerical Control (CNC) Planing Machine Operations

Manufacturing Production & Operations

Numerical Control (CNC) Set Up
Numerical Control (CNC) Set-Up Operations
Numerical Control (CNC) Turning Center
Planing
Planing Equipment
Planing Machine
Plastic
Plastic Work Pieces
Production Machinery
Profiling
Profiling Equipment
Profiling Machine
Prototype
Punch Press
Rod
Screw Machine
Screw Machine Operations
Shaping
Shaping Equipment
Shaping Machine
Shear Operations
Shears
Silicon
Swiss Screw Machine
Template
Thread
Threading Equipment
Threading Machine
Threading Operations
Titanium
Tool Design
Tools
Turn
Turning Center
Turning Equipment
Turning Machine
Turning Operations
Twin Spindle Lathe
Vertical Computer Numerical Control (CNC) Machine

Vertical Computer Numerical Control (CNC) Operation
Vertical Milling Machine
Water Jet
Welding
Wire

Additional KeyWords & KeyWord Phrases for Medical, Dental & Ophthalmic Laboratory Operations

Acrylic Paste
Acrylic Restoration
Adjustable Articulator
Alignment
American Academy of Orthotists & Prosthetists (AAOP)
American Board for Certification in Orthotics & Prosthetics (ABC)
American Dental Association (ADA)
Arch Support
Arcon Articulator
Articulator
Artificial Joint
Artificial Limb
Artificial Teeth
Balance
Biomechanical
Biomechanical Stability
Biomechanics
Bionoculars
Braces
Bridges
Brushes
Buffing
Buffing Wheel
Casting
Cement
Commission on Dental Accreditation (CDA)
Commission on Opticianry Accreditation (COA)
Contact Lenses
Contour
Conventional Lathe
Crown
Crucible
Crucible Former
Curvature
Cutting

Dental Accessories
Dental Appliance
Dental Appliance Technology
Dental Articulator
Dental Ceramics
Dental Elevator
Dental Finishing Disc
Dental Implant
Dental Inlay
Dental Laboratory (Lab)
Dental Laboratory (Lab) Bench Lathe
Dental Laboratory (Lab) Casting Machine
Dental Laboratory (Lab) Dental Prosthetics
Dental Laboratory (Lab) Furnace
Dental Laboratory (Lab) High-Speed Lathe
Dental Laboratory (Lab) Lathe
Dental Laboratory (Lab) Pressure Molding Device
Dental Laboratory (Lab) Pumise Lathe
Dental Laboratory (Lab) Technology
Dental Oven
Dental Polishing Disc
Dental Prosthesis
Dental Prosthetics
Dentures
Edging
Electric Burnout Furnace
Eyeglasses
Felt
Fitting
Flask Press
Forming
Full Dentures
Glass Lenses
Glasses
Grinder
Grinding
Hearing Aid
Impression
Inlay Furnace

Manufacturing Production & Operations

Inlays
Leather
Lens
Lens Blank
Lens Grinder
Lens Grinding
Lens Polisher
Lens Polishing
Lenses
Lensometer
Mechanics
Medical Anatomy
Medical Appliance
Medical Appliance Technology
Medical Device
Medical Laboratory (Lab)
Medical Laboratory (Lab) Device
Medical Laboratory (Lab) Equipment
Medical Laboratory (Lab) Materials
Medical Laboratory (Lab) Technology
Medical Supportive Device
Metal
Metal Finishing
Metal Forming
Metal Framework
Metal Restoration
Metal Surface
Micrometer
Model
Mold
Molding
National Association of Dental Laboratories (NADL)
National Board for Certification in Dental Technology (NBCERT)
National Commission on Orthotic & Prosthetic Education (NCOPE)
Nose Pad
Occlusion
Ophthalmic Anatomy
Ophthalmic Appliance
Ophthalmic Appliance Technology

Optical
Optical Assemblies
Optical Elements
Optical Instrumentation
Optical Instruments
Optical Mechanics
Opticianry
Optics
Oral Anatomy
Orthodontic Appliance
Orthodontic Implant
Orthodontic Prosthesis
Orthodontic Prosthetic
Orthodontic Technology
Orthodontics
Orthopedics
Orthoses
Orthotic & Prosthetic (O&P) Technology
Orthotic Device
Orthotic Technology
Orthotics
Partial Dentures
Patternmaking
Permanent Fixture
Pigment
Plaster
Plaster Mold
Plastic
Plastic Lenses
Polisher
Polishing
Porcelain
Porcelain Furnace
Porcelain Restoration
Porcelain Technology
Precision Optical Elements
Prescription Eyeglasses
Prescription Eyewear
Prophy Brushes

Manufacturing Production & Operations

Prostheses
Prosthetic
Prosthetic Device
Prosthetics Technology
Removal Dental Appliance
Removal Prosthodontics
Restorable Teeth
Restoration
Rubber
Semi-Adjustable Articulator
Shield
Surface
Surgical Appliance
Surgical Appliance Technology
Temple Pieces
Vision
Visual
Visual Anatomy
Wax
Wax Carver
Wax Spatula
Wax Teeth
Waxer
Wire Cutter

Additional KeyWords & KeyWord Phrases for Metal Refining Operations

Arc / Argon Oxygen Decarborization (ARC/AOD) Melter
Automatic Furnace
Cast
Casting
Coal
Coal Furnace
Control Room Operations
Direct Casing Operations
Electric Current
Electric Induction
Electric Melt Operations
Electric-Arc Furnace
Electric-Induction Furnace
Electricity
Fuel
Fuel Flow
Fuel Valve
Furnace
Furnace Operations
Furnace Temperature
Gas
Gas Furnace
Impurities
Impurity Strainer
Kettle
Kettle Operations
Melt Room
Melt Room Operations
Metal Cast
Metal Casting
Metal Color
Metal Fluidity
Metal-Refining Furnace
Metal-Refining Furnace Operations
Metals

Manufacturing Production & Operations

Metals Refining
Molding
Molding Machinery
Molds
Molten Metal
Oil
Oil Furnace
Open-Hearth Furnace
Oxygen Furnace
Steel
Steel Production
Strainer
Temperature
Temperature Adjustment
Temperature Management
Thermal
Thermal Chart
Thermal Instructions
Vessel
Vessel Operations
Water
Water Coolant

Additional KeyWords & KeyWord Phrases for Mixing & Blending Operations

Beverages
Blending
Blending Machine Operations
Chemical Blending
Chemical Mixing
Chemicals
Coating
Coating Operations
Color Pigment
Color Pigment Blending
Color Pigment Mixing
Compound
Dough Batter
Explosive Ingredient Blending
Explosive Ingredient Mixing
Explosive Ingredients
Explosives
Food
Food Products
Fruit Juices
Ink Blending
Ink Making
Liquid Ingredient Blending
Liquid Ingredient Mixing
Liquid Ingredients
Livestock Feed
Mixer
Mixing
Mixing Machine Operations
Spices
Tobacco
Tobacco Ingredient Blending
Tobacco Ingredient Mixing
Tobacco Ingredients

Manufacturing Production & Operations

Additional KeyWords & KeyWord Phrases for Photographic Processing Machine & Equipment Operations

You can use the words "photographic" and "photo" interchangeably.

Black & White (B&W)
Black & White (B&W) Photographic Processing
Bleach
Chemical Mixtures
Chemicals
Cleaning Solution
Color
Color Photographic Processing
Develop
Developing
Digital Photography
Digital Photography Operations
Digital Printing
Digital Printing Operations
Dye
Film
Film Processing
Finishing
Fixing
Negatives
Photographic
Photographic Laboratory (Lab) Management
Photographic Printing
Photographic Processing
Photographic Processing Equipment
Photographic Processing Equipment Operations
Photographic Processing Machine
Photographic Processing Machine Operations
Photography
Print
Printing Paper
Processing Solution

Rinsing Solution
Stop Bath
Touch Up
Ultrasonic
Ultrasonic Equipment
Ultrasonic Equipment Operation
Washes

Manufacturing Production & Operations

Additional KeyWords & KeyWord Phrases for Power Plant Operations & Distribution

American Public Power Association (APPA)
Auxiliary Operations
Auxiliary Power
Auxiliary Power Supply
Boiler
Boiler Operations
Boiler Operations Management
Circuit Breaker
Circuits
Connections
Control Area
Control Area Management
Control Area Operations
Control Center
Control Center Management
Control Center Operations
Control Management
Control Operations
Control Room Management
Control Room Operations
Coolant
Coolant Temperature
Crude Oil
Crude Oil Handling
Crude Oil Loading
Crude Oil Preparation
Crude Oil Pump
Crude Oil Pump Station
Crude Oil Pump System
Crude Oil Transfer
Crude Oil Unit
Crude Oil Unloading
Current
Current Converter
Current Routing

Distribution Operations
Distribution Operations Management
Distribution Systems
Distribution Systems Management
Electric Line
Electric Power Plant
Electric Power Station
Electric System Operations
Electric Systems
Electricity
Electricity Distribution
Electricity Flow
Emergency Planning
Emergency Preparedness
Emergency Response
Flux Level
Fossil Fuel
Fossil Fuel Handling
Fossil Fuel Loading
Fossil Fuel Preparation
Fossil Fuel Transfer
Fossil Fuel Unloading
Fossil-Fueled Power Plant
Gauges
Generator
Grid
Hazardous Materials (HAZMAT)
Hazardous Materials (HAZMAT) Disposal
Hazardous Materials (HAZMAT) Handling
Hazardous Materials (HAZMAT) Materials
Hazardous Materials (HAZMAT) Transportation
Hydrotreatment
Industrial Plant
International Brotherhood of Electrical Workers (IBEW)
Load
Load Dispatch
Load Management
Nuclear
Nuclear Control Operations

Manufacturing Production & Operations

Nuclear Control Room
Nuclear Control Room Operations
Nuclear Fuel
Nuclear Fuel Element
Nuclear Fuel Element Handling
Nuclear Fuel Element Loading
Nuclear Fuel Element Preparation
Nuclear Fuel Element Transfer
Nuclear Fuel Element Unloading
Nuclear Operations
Nuclear Plant
Nuclear Plant Operations
Nuclear Power
Nuclear Power Plant
Nuclear Power Reactor
Nuclear Power Reactor Operations
Nuclear Reactor
Nuclear Regulatory Commission (NRC)
Nuclear Station
Nuclear Station Operations
Oil
Oil Handling
Oil Loading
Oil Preparation
Oil Pump
Oil Pump Station
Oil Pump System
Oil Transfer
Oil Unloading
Petroleum
Petroleum Handling
Petroleum Loading
Petroleum Plant
Petroleum Plant Operations
Petroleum Preparation
Petroleum Pump
Petroleum Pump Station
Petroleum Pump System
Petroleum Transfer

Finding Needles in a Haystack

Petroleum Unloading
Pilot Board
Plant Control
Plant Control Management
Plant Control Operations
Plant Shut Down
Plant Start Up
Power
Power Demand
Power Flow
Power Flow Rate
Power Generating
Power Output
Power Plant
Power Plant Distribution
Power Plant Management
Power Plant Operations
Power Station
Power Supply
Power Systems
Power Systems Dispatch
Power Systems Management
Power Systems Operations
Power Yield
Power-Generating Equipment
Propulsion Plant
Pumper
Reactor
Reactor Operations
Reactor Period
Refinery
Refinery Operations
Shut Down
Start Up
Substation
Switches
System Operations
Temperature
Temperature Control

Manufacturing Production & Operations

Transformer
Transmission
Transmission Circuits
Transmission Grid
Transmission Network
Transmission Systems Operations
Turbine
Unit Operations
Unit Reactor
Unit Reactor Operations
Utilities
Valve
Voltage
Voltage Transformer

Additional KeyWords & KeyWord Phrases for Printing Machine Operations

Association for Suppliers of Printing, Publishing & Converting Technologies (NPES)
Conversion
Converting
Converting Technology
Cylinder
Desktop Operations
Desktop Printing
Desktop Printing Operations
Dies
Digital Press
Digital Printing
Drying Chamber
Electronic Prepress (EPP)
Electronic Prepress (EPP) Operations
Electronic Publishing
Electrostatic Printing
Etched Cylinder
Etched Plate
Feed Guide
Flexography
Gravure
High-Speed Digital Printing
High-Speed Press
High-Speed Printing
Ink
Ink Alignment
Ink Coverage
Ink Jet Printer
Ink Jet Printing
Ink Registration
In-Line Web Press
Laser Jet Printer
Laser Jet Printing
Letterpress

Manufacturing Production & Operations

Offset
Offset Lithography
Offset Press
Offset Press Operations
Page
Page Arrangement
Plate Adjustment
Plate Installation
Plate Making
Plate Mounting
Plate-Film Assemblies
Plateless Printing
Plate-Making Equipment
Plate-Making Machine
Plate-Making Technology
Plates
Prepress
Prepress Operations
Prepress Proofreading
Prepress Stripping
Press Cylinder
Press Operations
Printing
Printing Industry of America (PIA)
Printing Plate
Printing Press
Printing Press Operations
Printing-on-Demand
Publishing
Rollers
Rotary Printing
Screen Printing
Screens
Sheet-Fed Offset Press
Sheet-Fed Offset Press Operations
Specialty Printing
Stencil
Text
Text Composition

Text Positioning
Text Size
Text Style
Type
Typestyle
Variable Data Printing
Web Press
Web Press Operations

Manufacturing Production & Operations

Additional KeyWords & KeyWord Phrases for Quality & Inspection

Corrosion
Defects
Deviations
Engineering Defects
Equipment Audit
Equipment Inspection
Equipment Quality
Equipment Rejects
Fabrication Defects
Fault
Fault Analysis
Fault Isolation
Inspection
International Organization for Standardization (ISO 9000 / ISO 14000)
Manufacturing Defect Analyzer (MDA)
Manufacturing Defects
Material Rejects
Materials Audit
Materials Inspection
Materials Quality
Physical Inspection
Process
Product
Product Audit
Product Inspection
Product Quality
Product Rejects
Production Defects
Quality
Quality Assurance
Quality Assurance Audit
Quality Assurance Inspection
Quality Assurance Management
Quality Assurance Operations
Quality Audit

Quality Audit
Quality Control
Quality Control Audit
Quality Control Inspection
Quality Control Management
Quality Control Operations
Quality Engineering
Quality Inspection
Quality Management
Quality Operations
Rejection
Rejects
Rust
Total Quality Management (TQM)
Visual Inspection
Wear

Manufacturing Production & Operations

Additional KeyWords & KeyWord Phrases for Rolling Machine Operations

Breakdown Mill Operations
Calender Operations
Coils
Cold Mill Operations
Cold Milling Machine Operations
Dies
Flatten
Flattening Equipment
Flattening Machine
Flattening Machine Operations
Forming
Forming Equipment
Forming Machine
Forming Machine Operations
High-Frequency Mill Operations
High-Frequency Milling Machine Operations
Mandrel
Mill Operations
Milling Machine Operations
Piercer Operations
Reshaping
Roll Form
Roll Form Operations
Roll Forming
Rolling Machine
Rolling Machine Operations
Rolling Mechanisms
Rolls
Roughing Mill Operations
Sheet Metal
Steel
Steel Strip
Temper
Tempering Equipment
Tempering Machine

Tempering Machine Operations
Thickness
Thinning
Thinning Equipment
Thinning Machine
Thinning Machine Operations

Additional KeyWords & KeyWord Phrases for Saw Machine Operations

Backup Saw Operations
Band Saw
Band Saw Operations
Circular Saw
Circular Saw Operations
Crozer Machine
Crozer Machine Operations
Cut
Cutting
Edging
Knot Saw
Knot Saw Operations
Multi-Blade Sawing
Multi-Blade Sawing Machine
Multi-Blade Sawing Operations
Planing
Planing Equipment
Planing Machine
Planing Machine Operations
Resaw Operations
Rip Saw
Rip Saw Operations
Saw
Sawing
Sawing Machine Operations
Sawing Operations
Scroll Saw
Scroll Saw Operations

Additional KeyWords & KeyWord Phrases for Stationary Engineering, Boiler & Heating Equipment Operations

Air Conditioning
Air Conditioning System
Anneal
Batch Heat Treat Operations
Batch Operations
Baths
Bearings
Boiler
Boiler Design
Boiler Engineering
Boiler Operation
Building Owners & Managers Institute International (BOMI)
Chemistry
Compressor
Condenser
Corrosion
Current Frequency
Diesel Engine
Duct
Ductility
Electrical Power
Electrical Systems
Electricity
Electronic Induction Machine
Emissions
Emissions Control
Fire Safety System
Flame
Flame Temperature
Flame-Hardening Machine
Fuel
Fuel Consumption
Furnace
Furnace Operations

Manufacturing Production & Operations

Furnace Temperature
Gaskets
Generator
Harden
Hardness
Heat Cycle
Heat Cycle Requirements
Heat Treat
Heat Treat Operations
Heat Treating Furnace
Heating
Heating Cycle
Heating Duct
Heating Equipment
Heating System
Hydronic System
Hydronics
Induction
Induction Heating Coils
Induction Machines
International Union of Operating Engineers (IUOE)
Mechanical Systems
National Association of Power Engineers (NAPE)
Oil Brine Bath
Oven
Oven Operations
Plant Operating Engineering
Plant Operations
Plant Utilities
Plant Utilities Engineering
Power
Power Output
Power Yield
Pressure
Processing Sequence
Pump
Quenching Media
Refrigeration
Refrigeration System

Scarf & Anneal Operations
Soaking Pit
Stationary Engine
Stationary Engineering
Stationary Steam Engineering
Steam
Steam Pressure
Temper
Temperature
Temperature Adjustment
Thermal
Thermal Chart
Thermal Instructions
Toughness
Turbine
Utilities
Utility Operations
Vacuum
Vacuum Equipment
Ventilating
Ventilation
Ventilation System
Water
Water Bath
Water Vapor

Additional KeyWords & KeyWord Phrases for Tool & Die Making

Alloy
Boring
Ceramics
Composite Material
Composites
Coordinate Measuring Machines (CMM)
Diecasting
Dies
Drilling
Filing
Fixtures
Forging
Gauges
Grinding
Hardness
Heat Tolerance
Jigs
Lathes
Metals
Metal Molds
Metal Shaping
Metal-Forming Equipment
Metalworking
Plastics
Polishing
Special Guiding Device
Special Handling Device
Stamping
Tool & Die
Tool Programming
Tools

Additional KeyWords & KeyWord Phrases for Water & Liquid Waste Treatment Plant Operations

American Water Works Association (AWWA)
Biological
Biological Contaminant
Biological Laboratory Analysis
Biological Treatment
Biology
Chemical
Chemical Compound
Chemical Contaminant
Chemical Laboratory Analysis
Chemical Treatment
Chemical-Feeding Device
Chlorination
Chlorine
Chlorine Gas
Clean Water Act
Collection System
Community Water System
Emergency Planning
Emergency Preparedness
Emergency Response
Environmental Protection Agency (EPA)
Flow
Flow Measurement
Hazardous Materials (HAZMAT)
Industrial Liquid Waste
Industrial Liquid Waste Treatment
Industrial Liquid Waste Treatment Plant
Industrial Waste
Industrial Wastewater
Industrial Wastewater Plant
Industrial Wastewater Treatment
Irrigation
Laboratory (Lab) Analysis
Lake

Manufacturing Production & Operations

Liquid Waste
Liquid Waste Treatment
Liquid Waste Treatment Technology
Microbiological
Microbiology
Microorganism
Municipal Treatment Facility
Non-Community Water System
Nuclear
Nuclear Contaminant
Ocean
Oxygen
Pollutant
Pollution
Pollution Control
Public Health
Public Safety
Pump
Radioactive Contaminant
Radioactivity
River
Safe Drinking Water Act
Sample
Sample Analysis
Sample Collection
Sampling
Sedimentation
Sewage
Sewage System
Sludge
Sludge Disposal
Sludge Treatment
Stream
Treatment
Valves
Wastewater
Wastewater Treatment
Wastewater Treatment Technology
Water

Water Environment Federation (WEF)
Water Pollution
Water Treatment
Water Treatment Plan
Water Well
Well

Add Your Own Keywords & Keyword Phrases

Chapter 10

Public Relations & Public Affairs

Principal Keyword List:
Public Relations & Public Affairs

Representative Job Titles

Accredited Business Communicator (ABC)
Accredited in Public Relations (APR) Designation
Communications Analyst
Communications Director
Communications Manager
Communications Specialist
Community Relations Manager
Corporate Communications Director
Corporate Communications Manager
Corporate Spokesperson
Director of Communications
Director of Marketing & Public Relations
Director of Public Affairs
Director of Public Relations
Global Public Affairs Director
Global Public Affairs Manager
Global Public Affairs Representative
Global Public Relations Director
Global Public Relations Manager
Global Public Relations Representative
Government Affairs Representative
Government Relations Representative
Information & Communications Specialist
International Public Relations Director
International Public Relations Manager
International Public Relations Representative
Legislative Affairs Director
Legislative Affairs Manager
Lobbyist
Media Analyst
Media Outreach Coordinator
Media Outreach Specialist
Media Relations Director
Media Relations Manager
Media Relations Representative
Media Representative

Public Relations & Public Affairs

Media Specialist
Political Affairs Director
Political Affairs Manager
Political Affairs Representative
Political Affairs Specialist
Press Relations Director
Press Relations Manager
Press Relations Representative
Promotions Director
Promotions Manager
Public Affairs Director
Public Affairs Manager
Public Affairs Officer
Public Affairs Representative
Public Affairs Specialist
Public Information Officer
Public Information Specialist
Public Relations (PR) Account Executive
Public Relations (PR) Manager
Public Relations (PR) Representative
Public Relations (PR) Specialist
Public Relations Director
Public Relations Manager
Public Relations Specialist
Senior Vice President of Public Affairs
Senior Vice President of Public Relations
Spokesperson
Trade Show Manager
Vice President of Public Affairs
Vice President of Public Relations

Software, Systems & Technology

Active Data Online WebChat
Adobe Acrobat
Adobe Pagemaker
Astute Solutions PowerCenter
Atlas OnePoint GO TOAST
Austin Logistics CallSelect
Autodialing Systems
Avidian Technologies Prophet
Calling Line Identification Equipment
Click Tracks
Cognos 8 Business Intelligence
Corel WordPerfect
Databox
Dialed Number Identification Systems (DNIS)
Enterprise Resource Planning (ERP)
Epiphany
eStrate Softphone
Factiva
Fast Track Systems
FileMaker Pro
Focus
FrontRange Solutions Goldmine
Galilee Enterprise TargetPro
IBM DB2
IBM Lotus 1-2-3
IBM Lotus Notes
Informatica Corporation PowerCenter
Intellimed
Intuit QuickBooks
Key Survey
Khameleon Software E-Business Suite Special Edition
LexisNexis
Listserv
Mastermind
Microsoft Access
Microsoft Excel

Public Relations & Public Affairs

Microsoft Outlook
Microsoft PowerPoint
Microsoft Project
Microsoft Windows
Microsoft Word
MicroStrategy Desktop
Multi-Channel Contact Center Software
Nedstate Sitestat
NetSuite NetCRM
Parature eRealTime
Perseus Survey Solutions
Predictive Dialer
SAP
SAP Business One
SAS
Soffront CRM Portal
Software on Sailboats Desktop Sales Manager
SSA Global
Structured Query Language (SQL)
Sybase iAnywhere Pharma Anyware
Sybase iAnywhere Sales Anywhere
Sybase Structured Query Language (SQL)
TechExcel
Telemation e-CRM
Tigerpaw
Timpani Chat
Timpani Contact Center
Timpani Email
Unistat Statistical Package
Vanguard Sales Manager
Vantage MCIF
WebEx Sales Center
WinCross

KeyWords & KeyWord Phrases for Public Relations & Public Affairs

Account
Account Relationship Management
Account Retention
Account Services
Administration
Advertising
Advertising Communications
Advocacy
Alliance for Community Media (ACM)
Alliance for Competitive Communications (ACC)
American Communication Association (ACA)
Annual Report
Association for Progressive Communications (APC)
Awareness
Benefits & Features
Board of Directors
Board of Directors Communications
Board of Directors Relations
Brand
Brand Identity
Brand Integrity
Brand Positioning
Brand Strategy Development
Branding
Broadcast Journalism
Broadcast Media
Brochure Development
Brochures
Budget
Budget Administration
Budget Development
Budget Management
Budgeting
Business Building
Business Development

Catalogs
Citizen Outreach
Client Focus Groups
Client Inquiries
Client Interaction
Client Loyalty
Client Management
Client Relationship Management (CRM)
Client Retention
Client Satisfaction
Client Services
Clients
Communications
Communications
Communications Management
Communications Media
Communications Strategy
Community Affairs
Community Outreach
Community Relations
Computer Graphics
Computer Software
Computer Technology
Conference
Conference Management
Conference Planning
Consumer Awareness
Consumer Behavior
Consumer Brand
Consumer Buying Behavior
Consumer Public Affairs
Consumer Public Relations
Corporate Brand
Corporate Branding
Corporate Communications
Corporate Identity
Corporate Identity Campaign
Corporate Image
Corporate Image Campaign

Corporate Outreach
Corporate Vision
Creative Design
Creative Media
Creative Services
Creative Writing
Crisis Communications
Crisis Management
Cross-Cultural Communications
Customer
Customer Account
Customer Care
Customer Communications
Customer Feedback
Customer Focus Group
Customer Inquiries
Customer Interaction
Customer Loyalty
Customer Preferences
Customer Relationship Management (CRM)
Customer Retention
Customer Satisfaction
Customer Service
Customer Survey
Data
Data Analysis
Data Collection
Demographic Analysis
Desktop Publishing
Direct Mail
Direct Mail Pieces
Direct Response Pieces
Displays
E-Commerce
Economic Trends
Economics
Editing
Electronic Commerce
Electronic Journalism

Public Relations & Public Affairs

Electronic Media
Employee Affairs
Employee Communications
Employee Newsletters
Employee Relations
Endorsements
Event Management
Event Planning
Events
Exhibits
Expense Control
Expense Reporting
External Communications
Features & Benefits
Film Presentations
Focus Group
Fundraising
Global Markets
Goodwill
Government Affairs
Government Relations
Graphic Design
Grassroots
Grassroots Campaign
High-Impact Presentations
Incentive
Incentive Campaign
Incentive Planning
Industry Public Affairs
Industry Public Relations
Institute for Global Communications (IGC)
Internal Communications
International Association of Business Communicators (IABC)
International Communication Association (ICA)
Investor Communications
Issues
Issues Management
Journalism
Key Account Management

Key Account Relationship Management
Legislative Affairs
Legislative Affairs Management
Logistics
Management Communications
Market Research
Marketing Communications
Marketing Message
Media Affairs
Media Analysis
Media Events
Media Outreach
Media Packet
Media Presentation
Media Relations
Media Relations Management
Media Selection
Media Sourcing
Meeting Management
Meeting Planning
Meetings
Negotiation Tactics
Negotiations
New Business Development
New Market Development
New Market Identification
New Product Innovation
New Product Introduction
News
News Releases
Newsletters
Online Content Development
Personal Branding
Policies & Procedures
Political Action Committee (PAC)
Political Affairs
Political Affairs Management
Premiums
Presentations

Press Affairs
Press Conference
Press Relations
Press Relations Management
Press Releases
Print Communications
Print Journalism
Print Media
Private Branding
Product Demand
Product Innovation
Product Launch
Product Literature
Product Positioning
Product Promotions
Profit & Loss (P&L)
Profit & Loss (P&L) Management
Profit Growth
Profitability Analysis
Project
Project Administration
Project Management
Promotional Campaign
Promotional Displays
Promotions
Promotions Management
Psychographic Analysis
Public Affairs
Public Affairs Management
Public Affairs Programming
Public Appearances
Public Awareness
Public Information
Public Interest Groups
Public Opinion
Public Outreach
Public Relations
Public Relations (PR)
Public Relations (PR) Administration

Public Relations (PR) Management
Public Relations (PR) Principles
Public Relations (PR) Strategies
Public Relations (PR) Techniques
Public Relations Society of America (PRSA)
Publications
Publicity
Rebate
Recordkeeping
Relationship Management
Reporting
Research
Research & Development (R&D)
Return-on-Investment (ROI) Analysis
Sales Incentives
Scripts
Shareholder Communications
Shareholder Perceptions
Shareholder Relations
Shareholder Reports
Social Trends
Special Events
Special Events Management
Special Events Planning
Special Interest Group (SIG)
Speeches
Speechwriting
Sponsorship
Statistical Analysis
Statistics
Stockholder Communications
Stockholder Perceptions
Stockholder Relations
Stockholder Reports
Strategic Communications Plan
Strategic Customer Relationship Management
Strategic Growth
Strategic Planning
Strategic Positioning

Strategic Relationship Management
Survey
Survey Administration
Survey Design
Survey Interpretation
Survey Results
Surveys
Sweepstakes
Tactical Campaign
Team Building
Team Leadership
Technical Illustrations
Technical Writing
Trade Show Displays
Trade Show Management
Trade Shows
Training & Development
Trend Analysis
Trend Forecasting
Trends
Video Presentations
VIP Relations
Visual Communications
Website
Website Development
Website Management
Wholesale
Writing

Add Your Own Keywords & Keyword Phrases

Chapter 11

Purchasing

Principal Keyword List:

Purchasing

Representative Job Titles

Buyer
Accredited Purchasing Practitioner (APP)
Certified Professional Purchasing Manager (CPPM)
Certified Purchasing Manager (CPM)
Certified Purchasing Professional (CPP)
Commodities Buyer
Commodities Manager
Commodities Purchasing Agent
Contracts Administrator
Contracts Manager
Corporate Buyer
Corporate Purchasing Director
Department Buyer
Director of Acquisitions
Director of Materials
Director of Procurement
Director of Purchasing
Director of Strategic Sourcing
Field Purchasing Manager
Industrial Buyer
International Buyer
International Sourcing Agent
Materials Analyst
Materials Manager
Merchandise Manager
Procurement Assistant
Procurement Associate
Procurement Clerk
Procurement Manager
Procurement Officer
Procurement Specialist
Purchasing Agent
Purchasing Assistant
Purchasing Associate
Purchasing Clerk
Purchasing Director

Purchasing

Purchasing Manager
Purchasing Supervisor
Resource Manager
Retail Buyer
Senior Buyer
Senior Product Analyst
Subcontracts Administrator
Supplier Manager
Supply Chain Manager
Supply Manager
Trader
Vendor Purchasing Manager
Vendor Relations Manager
Vice President of Materials & Resources
Vice President of Purchasing
Wholesale Buyer

Software, Systems & Technology

Adobe Acrobat
Aestiva Purchase Order
Analytical Software
Ariba Spend Management Suite
Bill of Materials Software
BizTrack Business Solutions
Corel Paradox
Cost Estimating Software
Database Query Software
Database Software
Database User Interface Software
Document Management Software
Enterprise Resource Planning (ERP)
Epicor Vantage ERP
Graphic Presentation Software
IBM Lotus 1-2-3
IBM Lotus Notes
Intuit QuickBooks
JD Edwards EnterpriseOne Project Management
Keystroke POS
Kliger-Weiss Infosystems
Manufacturing Resources Planning Software
Material Safety Data Sheet (MSDS) Software
Materials Requirements Planning (MRP) Logistics Software
Materials Requirements Planning (MRP) Software
Materials Requirements Planning (MRP) Supply Chain Software
Microsoft Access
Microsoft Excel
Microsoft PowerPoint
Microsoft Project
Microsoft Windows
Microsoft Word
Millenium Software Atrex
Optical Character Reader (OCR) Software
Optical Character Scanning Software
Oracle Advanced Procurement

Purchasing

Oracle DBMS
Oracle Software
Point-of-Sale (POS)
Presentation Software
Primavera SureTrakProjectManager
Product Safety Documentation Software
Project Analysis & Costing Software
PurchasingNet eProcurement
Relational Database Software
Requirements Management Software
Sage Accpac
Sourcing Simulator
Spreadsheet Software
Supply Planning Multi-Site Material Planner
Windward System Five

KeyWords & KeyWord Phrases for Purchasing

Acquisition
Acquisition Management
Algebra
American Purchasing Society (APS)
Arithmetic
Barter
Barter Trade
Bid
Bid Proposals
Bid Reviews
Buy vs. Lease
Buying
Buying Trends
Calculus
Capital Equipment
Capital Equipment Acquisition
Claims
Commodities
Commodities Management
Commodities Purchasing
Competitive Bidding
Contract
Contract Administration
Contract Award
Contract Change Order
Contract Negotiation
Contract Terms & Conditions
Cradle-to-Grave Procurement
Cradle-to-Grave Purchasing
Demand
Demand Analysis
Demand Planning
Distribution
Distribution Management
Domestic Supplier

Durable Goods
Economic Ordering Quantity Methodology
Expediting
Fabricated Components
Fabricated Parts
Financial Analysis
Fixed-Price Contract
Foreign Supplier
Geometry
Goods & Services
Indefinite Price
Indefinite Quantity
Insourcing
Institute for Supply Management (ISM)
Integrated Logistics
Integrated Logistics Management (ILM)
Integrated Logistics Support (ILS)
Integrated Supply Chain
International Procurement
International Purchasing
International Sourcing
International Trade
Inventory
Inventory Control
Inventory Forecasting
Inventory Planning
Inventory Quantities
Invoice
Invoice Accuracy
Invoice Authorization
Invoice Processing
Invoice Review
Just-in-Time (JIT)
Just-in-Time (JIT) Inventory
Just-in-Time (JIT) Purchasing
Logistics
Logistics Management
Mark Down
Mark Up

Mark-Down Rates
Market Conditions
Mark-Up Rates
Materials Inspection
Materials Management
Materials Replenishment Ordering (MRO)
Materials Resource Planning (MRP)
Mathematics
Merchandise
Merchandise Management
Merchandise Movement
Merchandise Returns
National Association of Purchasing Management (NAPM)
Negotiations
Non-Durable Goods
Offshore
Offshore Purchasing
Order
Order Cancellations
Order Changes
Order Claims
Order Contracts
Order Expediting
Order Processing
Order Scheduling
Order Status
Outsourcing
Perishable Goods
Price
Price Analysis
Price Negotiations
Price Trends
Pricing
Private Label
Procurement
Procurement Management
Product Availability
Product Pricing
Product Reliability

Product Returns
Products
Proposal Review
Purchase
Purchase Order Cancellations
Purchase Order Changes
Purchase Order Claims
Purchase Order Contracts
Purchase Order Expediting
Purchase Order Processing
Purchase Order Scheduling
Purchase Order Status
Purchase Orders
Purchasing
Purchasing Contracts
Purchasing Management
Purchasing Specifications
Quality
Quality Inspection
Quality Review
Raw Materials
Regulations
Regulatory Compliance
Regulatory Review
Request for Proposal (RFP)
Request for Quotation (RFQ)
Requisition
Requisition
Requisition Order
Retail Buying
Retail Trade
Returns
Scheduling
Sourcing
Specifications
Specifications Compliance
Spreadsheet
Statistical Analysis
Statistics

Strategic Sourcing
Subcontractor
Subcontractor Negotiations
Supplier
Supplier Availability
Supplier Distribution Capabilities
Supplier Management
Supplier Negotiations
Supplier Quality
Supplier Reliability
Supplier Review
Supplier Selection
Supply Chain
Supply Chain Management
Supply Contract
Trade
Valuation
Value
Vendor Negotiations
Vendor Partnerships
Vendor Purchasing
Vendor Purchasing Management
Vendor Quality
Vendor Quality Certification
Vendor Selection
Warehouse
Warehousing
Wholesale Buying
Wholesale Trade
Yield

Add Your Own Keywords & Keyword Phrases

Chapter 12

Security

Principal Keyword List:

Corporate, Industrial & Personal Security

Representative Job Titles

Background Investigator
Certified Legal Investigator (CLI)
Corporate Security Manager
Corporate Security Officer
Criminal Investigator
Detective
Director of Corporate Security
Director of Industrial Security
Investigator
Loss Prevention Agent
Loss Prevention Associate
Loss Prevention Detective
Loss Prevention Investigator
Loss Prevention Manager
Loss Prevention Officer
Loss Prevention Specialist
Pre-Employment Investigator
Private Detective
Private Investigator
Security Guard
Security Officer
Store Detective
Undercover Investigator
Vice President of Corporate Security
Vice President of Industrial Security
Vice President of Safety

Software, Systems & Technology

Administrative Software
Adobe Acrobat
Blumberg Drafting Libraries
Corel WordPerfect
Data Entry Software
Database Query Software
Database Software
dBase Plus
Digital Contracts
FileMaker Pro
IBM Lotus 1-2-3
IBM Lotus Notes
Intuit QuickBooks
Legal MacPac
Legal Terminology Software
LexisNexis
LexisNexis CheckCite
LexisNexis Total Search
Medical Terminology Software
Microsoft Access
Microsoft Excel
Microsoft Outlook
Microsoft PowerPoint
Microsoft Project
Microsoft Windows
Microsoft Word
Presentation Software
Project Management Software
Scientific Terminology Software
Spreadsheet Software
Technical Terminology Software
Thomson West FindLaw
Uniscribe
Westlaw

Keywords & Keyword Phrases for Corporate, Industrial & Personal Security

Alarm
Alarm Response
Alarm Systems
American Society for Industrial Security International (ASISI)
Appeals
Appeals Process
Apprehension
Assault
Asset Protection
Asset Recovery
Assets
Audio
Audio Equipment
Audio Surveillance
Audio Surveillance Technology
Audio Technology
Background Investigation
Building Inspection
Building Security
Burglary
Case
Case Management
Case Reporting
Cash
Cash Control
Cash Protection
Casino
Casino Operations
Casino Security
Celebrity Protection
Celebrity Security
Closed-Circuit Camera
Closed-Circuit Surveillance
Community Outreach
Corporate Fraud

Corporate Protection
Corporate Protective Detail
Corporate Protective Service
Corporate Security
Credit Report
Crime
Criminal
Criminal Activity
Criminal Apprehension
Criminal History
Criminal Investigation
Crisis
Crisis Communications
Crisis Response
Damage
Detection
Doors
Electronic Detection
Electronic Security
Electronic Security System
Electronic Surveillance
Emergency
Emergency Planning
Emergency Preparedness
Emergency Response
Employee Protection
Employee Safety
Employee Welfare
Employment Verification
Executive Protection
Executive Security
Explosives
Explosives Screening
External Investigation
Facilities
Facilities Protection
Facilities Security
Financial Investigation
Fire Prevention

First Aid
Freight Protection
Freight Security
Gaming
Gaming Investigation
Gaming Operations
Gaming Surveillance
Gates
Homicide
Hotel
Hotel Security
Identification
Incident Response
Industrial Espionage
Industrial Protection
Industrial Security
Information Protection
Information Security
Inspection
Intellectual Property
Internal Investigation
Interrogation
Intruder
Intrusion
Investigation
Investigations Management
Law Enforcement
Legal Investigation
License
Loss Control
Loss Prevention
Loss Prevention Investigation
Loss Prevention Management
Media Affairs
Media Relations
Medical Response
Merchandise Control
Metal Detectors
Missing Persons

Security

Mobile Patrol
National Association of Legal Investigators (NALI)
Package Inspection
Patrol
Perimeter
Personal Protection
Personal Security
Physical Security
Physical Surveillance
Police Science
Pre-Employment Check
Pre-Employment Investigation
Pre-Employment Verification
Premarital Investigation
Premarital Screening
Press Affairs
Press Relations
Private Investigation
Private Investigator (PI) License
Prohibited Area
Property Damage
Property Protection
Property Security
Protection
Protective Detail
Protective Service
Public Affairs
Public Relations
Public Safety
Radio Communications
Radio-to-Radio Communications
Retail Security
Risk
Risk Assessment
Risk Management
Robbery
Safety
Safety Management
Safety Operations

Safety Training
Screening
Search
Search & Seizure
Secure
Secure Facilities
Secure Premises
Security
Security Alarm
Security Investigations
Security Operations
Security Patrol
Seizure
Site Security
Still Camera
Store Security
Suicide
Surveillance
Surveillance Systems
Surveillance Technology
Suspect
Suspicious Act
Suspicious Behavior
Tactical Field Operations
Telephone Communications
Terrorism
Terrorism Prevention
Terrorism Threat
Terrorist
Terrorist Threat
Theft
Theft Investigation
Theft Prevention
Traffic
Traffic Violation
Traffic Violation Warning
Unauthorized Personnel
Undercover
Undercover Investigation

Undercover Operation
Undercover Surveillance
Unlawful Acts
Vandalism
Vandalism Prevention
Video
Video Camera
Video Equipment
Video Surveillance
Video Surveillance Technology
Video Technology
Violation
VIP Protection
VIP Security
Weapons
Weapons Certification
Weapons Handling
Weapons Screening
White-Collar Crime
Will
Windows
Workers' Compensation
Workers' Compensation Investigation

Add Your Own Keywords & Keyword Phrases

Chapter 13

Translation & Interpretation

Principal Keyword List:
Translation & Interpretation

Representative Job Titles

Bilingual Interpreter
Bilingual Translator
Conference Interpreter
Conference Translator
Consecutive Interpreter
Consecutive Translator
Court Interpreter
Court Translator
Deaf-to-Deaf Interpreter
Educational Interpreter
Educational Translator
Escort Interpreter
Escort Translator
Foreign Language Interpreter
Foreign Language Linguist
Foreign Language Translator
Guide Interpreter
Interpreter
Judiciary Interpreter
Judiciary Translator
Legal Interpreter
Legal Translator
Linguist
Literary Translator
Localization Translator
Medical Interpreter
Medical Translator
Oral Interpreter
Oral Translator
Paraprofessional Interpreter
Sign Language Interpreter
Simultaneous Interpreter
Translator

Software, Systems & Technology

Adams Globalization LT Manager
Adobe Acrobat
Adobe Illustrator
Adobe Pagemaker
Adobe Photoshop
Alchemy Software Development Catalyst
Allis Technologies Batam
Applied Information Technologies Visual Localize
Austraat Globalization Solutions Globalization Image Assistant
Basis Technology Rosette Globalization Platform
Convey Software Localization Suite
Corel WordPerfect
Database Administration Software
Database Query Software
Database Software
Digital Sonata Carabao Language Kit
FileMaker Pro
Freelang Software
GlobaWare International SIAT
Glossy
Google Translation Gadget
IBM Lotus 1-2-3
IBM Lotus Notes
Idiom WorldServer
iLanguage Global eBuild
Intuit QuickBooks
Language Automation WebPlexer
Language Weaver
Lingobit Technologies Lingobit Localizer
Lingotek
Lingvistica PARS Translation
Lingvosoft Software
Lionbridge Technologies LionStream
Microsoft Access
Microsoft Excel
Microsoft Office

Microsoft Outlook
Microsoft PowerPoint
Microsoft Project
Microsoft Windows
Microsoft Word
Multilizer 5.0
PARS Professional Software
planetarySales.com Global eBusiness System
Project Management Software
RapidSolution Software RapidTranslation 4.0
SDL International Enterprise Translation Server
SDL WebFlow
Skandis Systems WebGlobalization
Smart Link @prompt Expert
Smart Link @prompt Professional
Spreadsheet Software
SYSTRAN Enterprise
thebigword TranzManager
Trados Corporate Translation Solution
Translations.com GlobalLink GMS
Trans-Project Office
VerbumSoft QuickCount
Welocalize XTEND Globalization Management Suite
WhiteSmoke
Xanadu

Keywords & Keyword Phrases for Translation & Interpretation

Only the most-commonly used languages have been included in this list. Refer to an online directory for a listing of the more than 2000 languages spoken worldwide.

Active Language
Afrikaans
Afro-Asiatic Languages
Altaic Languages
American Dialect Society (ADS)
American Literary Translators Association (ALTA)
American Sign Language (ASL)
American Translators Association (ATA)
Analysis
Arabic
Asian Languages
Austro-Asiatic Languages
Austronesian Languages
Baltic Languages
Bantu Languages
Behaviors
Bengali
Bilingual Interpretation
Bilingual Translation
Cantonese
Caucasian Languages
Celtic Languages
Chinese
Colloquial Terminology
Colloquialism
Communications
Composition
Computerized Terminology Bank
Concepts
Conference Interpretation
Conference Translation
Confidentiality

Consecutive Interpretation
Consecutive Translation
Contact Languages
Contact Signing
Court Interpretation
Court Translation
Croatian
Cross-Cultural Communications
Cross-Cultural Relations
Cultural Nuances
Cultural References
Danish
Deaf-to-Deaf Interpretation
Deaf-to-Deaf Interpreting
Dictionaries
Dravidian Languages
Dutch
Editing
Educational Interpretation
Educational Translation
Egyptian
Encyclopedias
English
Eskimo
Esperanto
European Language Resources Association (ELRA)
Finger Spelling
Finnish
Flemish
Foreign Culture
Foreign Language
Foreign Language Dictionaries
Foreign Language Glossaries
Foreign Language Interpretation
Foreign Language Translation
French
Gaelic
German
Germanic Languages

Translation & Interpretation

Glossaries
Grammar
Grammatical Rules
Greek
Gujarati
Hand Signs
Hawaiian
Hebrew
Hindi
Historical Context
Hungarian
Icelandic
Idiom
Indo-European Languages
Indo-Iranian Languages
International Business
International Diplomacy
Irish
Italian
Italic Languages
Japanese
Judiciary Interpretation
Judiciary Translation
Kannada
Korean
Kurdish
Language
Language Combination
Latin
Legal Interpretation
Legal Translation
Lexicons
Literary Translation
Localization
Localization Industry Standards Association (LISA)
Localization Translation
Machine-Assisted Translation
Malayalam
Mandarin Chinese

Marathi
Medical Interpretation
Medical Translation
Memory Tools
Mental Dexterity
National Association of Judiciary Interpreters & Translators (NAJIT)
National Association of the Deaf (NAD)
Native Language
Native Tongue
Niger-Congo Languages
Non-Native Language
Non-Native Tongue
North American Native Languages
Norwegian
Oral Interpretation
Oral Interpreting
Oral Translation
Oriya
Passive Language
Phrases
Polish
Portuguese
Punjabi
Registry of Interpreters for the Deaf (RID)
Romance Languages
Romanian
Russian
Sanskrit
Secondary Language
Sentence Structure
Sign Language
Sign Language Interpretation
Signing
Simultaneous Interpretation
Simultaneous Translation
Sino-Tibetan Languages
Slavic Languages
Software Localization
Source Language

Translation & Interpretation

Spanish
Subject Matter
Swahili
Swedish
Tactile Signing
Tamil
Target Language
Technology Localization
Telugu
Terminology
Text
Text Interpretation
Text Translation
Textual Analysis
Thai
Translators and Interpreters Guild (TIG)
Transliterate
Turkish
Verbal Interpretation
Verbal Interpreting
Verbal Translation
Vietnamese
Words
Writing
Writing Style
Written Interpretation
Written Interpreting
Written Translation
Yiddish

Add Your Own Keywords & Keyword Phrases

Chapter 14

Transportation, Logistics, Warehousing & Distribution

Principal Keyword List:
Transportation (Aviation, Maritime, Rail, Trucking), Logistics, Warehousing & Distribution

Additional Keyword Lists:
Air Transportation
Air Transportation: Air Traffic Control
Air Transportation: Aircraft Cargo Handling
Air Transportation: Airfield Operations
Air Transportation: Pilots, Copilots & Flight Engineers
Aviation Inspection
Logistics
Maritime Transportation
Rail Transportation
Trucking
Warehouse & Distribution Management

Representative Job Titles

Air Traffic Control Specialist (ATCS)
Air Traffic Controller
Aircraft Cargo Handling Manager
Aircraft Cargo Handling Operations Manager
Aircraft Cargo Handling Supervisor
Aircraft Dispatcher
Aircraft Inspector
Aircraft Quality Assurance Inspector
Aircraft Quality Control Inspector
Aircraft Systems Inspector
Airfield Manager
Airfield Operations Coordinator
Airfield Operations Manager
Airfield Operations Officer
Airfield Operations Specialist
Airfield Operations Superintendent
Airfield Operations Supervisor
Airline Captain
Airline Copilot
Airline Pilot
Airline Transport Pilot
Airport Manager
Airport Operations Coordinator
Airport Operations Manager
Airport Operations Officer
Airport Operations Specialist
Airport Operations Superintendent
Airport Operations Supervisor
Airport Tower Controller
Airworthiness Safety Inspector
Aviation Inspector
Aviation Maintenance Inspector
Aviation Safety Inspector
Avionics Safety Inspector
Baggage Manager
Baggage Supervisor

Transportation, Logistics, Warehousing & Distribution

Barge Engineer
Boat Captain
Boat Engineer
Boat Pilot
Bulk Delivery Driver
Bulk Delivery Truck Driver
Calibration
Cantilever Truck Driver
Captain
Cargo Agent
Cargo Manager
Cargo Supervisor
Certified Professional Controller (CPC)
Charter Boat Captain
Charter Boat Pilot
Charter Pilot
Check Airman
City Driver
Cold Storage Manager
Cold Storage Supervisor
Commercial Aircraft Pilot
Commercial Airplane Pilot
Commercial Helicopter Pilot
Commercial Pilot
Commuter Pilot
Conductor
Copilot
Cruise Ship Captain
Deckhand
Delivery Driver
Delivery Truck Driver
Diesel-Electric Locomotive Engineer
Dinkey Operator
Director of Dispatch Operations
Director of Distribution
Director of Logistics
Director of Operations
Director of Transportation
Dispatch Manager

Dispatch Operations Manager
Dispatcher
Distribution Manager
Distribution Operations Manager
Distribution Supervisor
Docking Master
Docking Pilot
Document Manager
Documentation Clerk
Driver
Drop Shipment Clerk
Electric Locomotive Engineer
Electrical Systems Engineer
Emergency Medical Services (EMS) Helicopter Pilot
Engineer
Enroute Controller
Equipment Service Lead
Facilities Manager
Feeder Driver
Ferry Boat Captain
Ferry Boat Engineer
Ferry Boat Pilot
Ferry Engineer
First Officer
Flatbed Truck Driver
Fleet Administrator
Fleet Manager
Fleet Operations Manager
Flight Engineer
Flight Operations Director
Flight Operations Manager
Forklift Driver
Forklift Operator
Freight Agent
Freight Broker
Freight Coordinator
Freight Locomotive Engineer
Freight Operations Manager
Gas Locomotive Engineer

Transportation, Logistics, Warehousing & Distribution

Ground Controller
Ground Operations Manager
Ground Operations Supervisor
Harbor Engineer
Harbor Tug Captain
Harbor Tug Engineer
Harbor Tug Pilot
Harbor Tugboat Captain
Harbor Tugboat Engineer
Harbor Tugboat Pilot
Helicopter Copilot
Helicopter Pilot
High-Lift Order Picker Truck Driver
Inland Marine Towing Vessel Engineer
Integrated Logistics Management (ILM) Manager
Integrated Logistics Support (ILS) Manager
Inventory Manager
Inventory Planner
Inventory Supervisor
Lift Truck Driver
Line Haul Driver
Line Haul Truck Driver
Line Pilot
Line Service Supervisor
Load Out Manager
Load Out Supervisor
Load Planner
Loadmaster
Locomotive Engineer
Locomotive Technician
Logistician
Logistics Analyst
Logistics Coordinator
Logistics Engineer
Logistics Management Specialist
Logistics Manager
Logistics Operations Manager
Logistics Service Representative
Logistics Supervisor

Logistics System Engineer
Logistics Team Lead
Marine Pilot
Marine Vessel Operator
Material Handler
Materials Manager
Materials Operations Manager
Mobile Airfield Coordinator
Mobile Airfield Manager
Mobile Airfield Specialist
Mobile Airfield Superintendent
Operations Agent
Operations Manager
Operations Specialist
Operations Supervisor
Over-the-Road (OTR) Driver
Over-the-Road (OTR) Truck Driver
Owner Operator
Package Car Driver
Package Delivery Driver
Parts Manager
Parts Operations Manager
Passenger Locomotive Engineer
Pick-Up & Delivery Driver
Pilot
Platform Lift Truck Driver
Port Engineer
Private Pilot
Propulsion Engineer
Rail Operations Controller
Rail Operations Dispatcher
Rail Operations Manager
Railroad Conductor
Railroad Engineer
Ramp Manager
Ramp Operations Manager
Ramp Operations Supervisor
Ramp Supervisor
Reach-Type Outrigger Truck Driver

Transportation, Logistics, Warehousing & Distribution

Receiving Clerk
Receiving Manager
Receiving Operations Manager
Receiving Supervisor
River Pilot
Road Driver
Route Driver
Route Manager
Route Supervisor
Route Truck Driver
Routing Manager
Routing Supervisor
Run Driver
Run Truck Driver
Safety Manager
Safety Operations Manager
Shag Truck Driver
Ship Broker
Ship Captain
Ship Engineer
Ship Pilot
Shipping & Receiving Clerk
Shipping & Receiving Manager
Shipping & Receiving Operations Manager
Shipping & Receiving Supervisor
Shipping Clerk
Shipping Manager
Shipping Supervisor
Sort Operations Leader
Sort Operations Manager
Spotter Driver
Steam Locomotive Engineer
Stockroom Manager
Stockroom Supervisor
Storage Manager
Storage Supervisor
Stores Manager
Stores Supervisor
Supply Chain Manager

Supply Manager
Technical Inspector
Terminal Controller
Terminal Manager
Terminal Operations Manager
Terminal Operator
Towboat Captain
Towboat Engineer
Towboat Pilot
Track Inspector
Tractor-Trailer Driver
Traffic Analyst
Traffic Clerk
Traffic Manager
Traffic Operations Manager
Traffic Planner
Traffic Technician
Train Dispatcher
Train Engineer
Train Operations Manager
Train Operations Supervisor
Trainmaster
Transportation Manager
Transportation Manager
Transportation Operations Manager
Transportation Planner
Transportation Supervisor
Truck Dispatcher
Truck Driver
Trucker
Tug Captain
Tug Engineer
Tug Pilot
Tugboat Captain
Tugboat Engineer
Tugboat Pilot
Turbine Locomotive Engineer
Utility Driver
Utility Truck Driver

Transportation, Logistics, Warehousing & Distribution

Vehicle Dispatcher
Vice President of Distribution
Vice President of Transportation
Vice President of Warehousing
Warehouse Manager
Warehouse Operations Manager
Warehouse Supervisor
Warehouseman
Yardmaster

Software, Systems & Technology

ABOL Manifest Systems
ADi SmartBOL
Adobe Acrobat
AeroPlanner
Aestiva Purchase Order
Aileron Trim Switches
Aircraft Data Loaders
Airline Pilots Daily Aviation Log PPC
AirSmith FlightPrompt
Air-Track Cloudberry
Aljex Inventory
ALK Technologies FleetSuite
ALK Technologies PC*Miller
Attitude Heading Reference Systems (AHRS)
Automatic Direction Finder (ADF) Radio Systems
Automatic Landing Systems
Autopilot Systems
AXSDry
AXSLiner
AXSMarine
AXSTanker
Bar Code Labeling Software
Bassnet Fleet Management System
Bentley Transportation Data Manager
Bornemann Associates Flight Plan
Computer-Aided Dispatching Auto Routing Systems
CoPilot Truck
Data Load Selectors
Digital Communication Display Units (DCDU)
DM2 Bills of Lading
Dockmaster
Dolphin Maritime
Easy Trucker
Endicia Internet Postage
Enterprise Resource Planning (ERP) Software
Enterprise Systems RFID Data Management

Transportation, Logistics, Warehousing & Distribution

ESRI ArcIMS
FileMaker Pro
Fixed Radio Frequency Identification Device (RFID) Readers
Flight Database Systems
Fog Line Software Truckn2004
FreightDATA
Global Information System (GIS)
Global Positioning System (GPS)
High-Frequency (HF) Radio Communication Systems
HighJump Software Warehouse Advantage
Hydraulic Actuators
Hydraulic Control Systems
Hydraulic Pressure Regulators
IBM i2 Transportation Manager
IBM Lotus 1-2-3
IBM Lotus Notes
IFT-Pro
IMSure Solutions SHIPflex
Infosite Technologies DM Warehousing
Integrated Decision Support Corporation Expert Fuel
Integrated Decision Support Corporation Match Advice
Integrated Decision Support Corporation Netwise Enterprise
Integrated Decision Support Corporation Netwise Frontline
Integrated Decision Support Corporation Netwise Supply Chain
Integrated Decision Support Corporation Route Advice
Intergraph GeoMedia Transportation Manager
Labelmaster Software REG-Trieve
Laser Substrates PostalXport
MacroSoft Quo Vadis
Maritime Software Suite
Microsoft Access
Microsoft Excel
Microsoft Outlook
Microsoft PowerPoint
Microsoft Project
Microsoft Windows
Microsoft Word
MRA Technologies MRATrack Warehouse Management System
MSR Visual Exporter Document Library

Navzilla
NetPas
NOTAM-D Development Airport Insight
Ocean Portal
PC Chartplanner
QUALCOMM QTRACS
QUALCOMM ViaWeb
Radio Frequency Identification Device (RFID)
RMS Flitesoft
Rudder Trim Knobs
Sabre
SBS International Maestro Suite
Sentai Pinpoint
Sentai WarehouseTrac
Situation Resources Tracking Software
Sky Scheduler
Skylog Services Skylog Pro
Summary Systems Fleet Commander
TECSYS EliteSeries
TECSYS PointForce Enterprise
TMW PowerSuite
Transportation Management Software
Truckers Helper
Varsity ShipSoft Chain Execution Suite
Vehicular Global Positioning System (GPS)
WindowBook Postage Package Partner

KeyWords & KeyWord Phrases for Transportation (Aviation, Maritime, Rail, Truck), Logistics, Warehousing & Distribution

Agency Operations
Air Brakes
Air Pressure
Airline
Airline Cargo
Airline Freight
Airline Terminal
American Public Transport Association (APTA)
Amperage
Arithmetic
Asset Management
Baggage
Baggage Weight
Bar Code Scanner
Bar Code Scanning
Bar Codes
Bar Coding
Bills of Lading
Calculus
Cargo
Cargo Arrival
Cargo Classification
Cargo Consolidation
Cargo Contents
Cargo Delivery
Cargo Handling
Cargo Movement
Cargo Pick-Up
Cargo Rates
Cargo Shipment
Cargo Transport
Cargo Weight
Carrier
Carrier Management

Certified Records
Certified Reports
Common Carrier
Consignee
Consignment
Consolidation
Container Transportation
Contract Transportation Service
Crisis Management
Crisis Response
Customer Delivery
Dedicated Logistics
Delivery
Delivery Instructions
Delivery Operations
Demurrage
Demurrage Charges
Department of Transportation (DOT)
Dispatch
Dispatch Management
Dispatch Operations
Dispatch Operations Management
Dispatching
Distribution
Distribution Management
Document Management
Document Preparation
Documentation
Driver Leasing
Emergency Planning & Preparedness
Emergency Response
Equipment
Equipment Control
Equipment Dispatch
Equipment Maintenance
Equipment Repair
Expediting
Export
Export Documentation

Transportation, Logistics, Warehousing & Distribution

Facilities
Facilities Management
Fees
Fleet
Fleet Management
Fleet Operations
Fleet Operations Management
Freight
Freight Arrival
Freight Classification
Freight Company
Freight Consolidation
Freight Contents
Freight Delivery
Freight Forwarding
Freight Movement
Freight Operations
Freight Operations Management
Freight Pick-Up
Freight Rates
Freight Shipment
Freight Shipping
Freight Weight
Gauges
Geometry
Goods
Goods Transportation
Import
Import Documentation
Import/Export Documentation
Inbound
Inbound Transportation
Incident Reporting
Incoming Shipment
Incoming Shipping Records
Institute for Transportation Research & Education (ITRE)
Institute of Transportation Engineers (ITE)
Integrated Logistics
Integrated Logistics Management

Integrated Logistics Support (ILS)
Intermodal
Intermodal Dispatch
Intermodal Dispatcher
Intermodal Transportation Network
International Institute of Transportation Engineers (IITE)
Line Management
Load
Load Analysis
Load Planning
Loading
Loading Platform
Logistics
Logistics Management
Logistics Services
Mail
Mail Cargo
Mail Freight
Mail Transportation
Mail Weight
Maintenance
Maintenance & Repair
Manifest
Maritime Operations
Materials
Materials Assembly
Materials Dispatch
Materials Movement
Materials Receiving
Materials Recording
Materials Resource Planning (MRP)
Materials Shipment
Materials Shipping
Materials Unpacking
Materials Verification
Merchandise
Merchandise Assembly
Merchandise Dispatch
Merchandise Movement

Transportation, Logistics, Warehousing & Distribution

Merchandise Receiving
Merchandise Recording
Merchandise Shipping
Merchandise Unpacking
Merchandise Verification
Meter
Object Scanning
Object Scanning Device
Order
Order Processing
Order Receiving
Order Shipment
Order Shipping
Order Verification
Outbound
Outbound Transportation
Outgoing Shipment
Outgoing Shipping Records
Over-The-Road (OTR) Transportation
Package
Package Scale
Passengers
Pick-Up
Pick-Up Operations
Port
Port Operations
Postal Rates
Rate Calculations
Rates
Receiving
Receiving Clerk
Receiving Management
Receiving Manager
Receiving Operations
Regulations
Regulatory Affairs
Regulatory Compliance
Regulatory Reporting
Repair

Route
Route Analysis
Route Management
Route Planning
Routing
Routing Management
Safety
Safety Equipment
Safety Management
Safety Operations
Safety Training
Scales
Schedule
Scheduling
Shipment
Shipment Data
Shipment Tracing
Shipper
Shipping
Shipping & Receiving
Shipping & Receiving Management
Shipping & Receiving Operations
Shipping & Receiving Operations Management
Shipping Cargo
Shipping Charge
Shipping Company
Shipping Dock
Shipping Documentation
Shipping Fees
Shipping Freight
Shipping Instructions
Shipping Management
Shipping Materials
Shipping Order
Shipping Procedures
Shipping Rates
Shipping Routes
Shipping Tariffs
Shortage

Transportation, Logistics, Warehousing & Distribution

Space Availability
Space Layout
Space Planning
Speed
Statistical Analysis
Statistics
Tariff
Tariff Coding
Tariff Coding System
Tariff Group
Terminal Operations
Throttle
Traffic
Traffic Management
Traffic Operations
Traffic Operations Management
Traffic Planning
Train
Train Cargo
Train Freight
Train Terminal
Transportation
Transportation Management
Transportation Operations
Transportation Operations Management
Transportation Planning
Transportation Research Board (TRB)
Truck
Truck Cargo
Truck Freight
Truck Terminal
Trucking
US Department of Transportation (DOT)
Vehicle
Vehicle Dispatch
Weight
Weight & Balance
Weight & Balance Calculation
Work Order

Worker Dispatch
Workflow Optimization

Additional Keywords & Keyword Phrases for Air Transportation

Air Line Pilots Association (ALPA)
Air Service
Air Traffic
Air Traffic Control
Air Traffic Control Station
Air Transport Association of America (ATAA)
Aircraft
Aircraft Maintenance
Aircraft Repair
Aircraft Service Operations
Airline
Airport
Airport Emergency Services
Airport Management
Airport Operations
Airport Operations Management
Airspace
Air-to-Ground
Air-to-Ground Radio
Air-to-Ground Radio Communications
Air-to-Ground Radio Contact
Air-to-Ground Radio Transmission
Altitude
American Association of Airport Executives (AAAE)
Arrival
Arriving Flight
Aviation
Charts
Commercial Aircraft
Commercial Airline
Delay
Departing Flight
Departure
Designated Airspace
Direction

Emergency Landing
Emergency Management
Emergency Planning
Emergency Response
Enroute Control
Federal Aviation Administration (FAA)
Flight
Flight Delay
Flight Engineering
Flight Instruction
Flight Instruments
Flight Log
Flight Operations
Flight Operations Publications
Flight Plan
Flight Planning
Flight Planning Publications
Flight Record
Flight Schedule
Flying Hours
Fuel
Fuel Supply
Fuselage
Ground Control
Helicopter
Helicopter Association International (HAI)
Inflight
International Civil Aviation Organization (ICAO)
Landing
Landing Approach
License
Maps
National Airspace System (NSA)
National Airspace System (NSA) Architecture
Passenger Services
Passengers
Pilot's License
Point-to-Point Radio Communications
Point-to-Point Radio Contact

Point-to-Point Radio Transmission
Preflight
Private Aircraft
Runway
Search & Rescue
Speed
Taxiway
Traffic Control
Ultra High-Frequency (UHF) Radio Communication System
Velocity
Very High-Frequency (VHF) Direction Finder
Very High-Frequency (VHF) Omni-Directional Radio Range VOR Navigation Systems
Very High-Frequency (VHF) Radio Communication System
Visibility
Visual Observation
Weather
Weather Conditions
Weight & Balance
Wind Velocity

Additional Keywords & Keyword Phrases for Air Traffic Control

Air Traffic
Air Traffic Control
Air Traffic Control Center
Air Traffic Controller (Enroute Option)
Air Traffic Controller (Tower Option)
Air Traffic Movement
Altitude
Altitude Sector
Arrival Instructions
Baggage Handling Vehicle Traffic
Commercial Airline Flight
Commercial Airline Routing
Control Center
FAA Air Traffic Collegiate Training Initiative Program
Flight Path
Flight Plan
Flight Safety
Flight Traffic
Flight Vector
Ground Traffic
Landing
Landing Aids
Landing Authorization
Landing Clearance
Landing Instructions
Maintenance Vehicle Traffic
National Air Traffic Controllers Association (NATCA)
Navigation
Navigational Aids
Private Aircraft Flight
Private Aircraft Routing
Radar
Takeoff
Takeoff Authorization
Takeoff Clearance

Transportation, Logistics, Warehousing & Distribution

Takeoff Instructions
Taxiing
Taxiing Aircraft
Traffic Pattern
Ultra High-Frequency (UHF) Radio Communication System
Vector
Very High-Frequency (VHF) Direction Finder
Very High-Frequency (VHF) Omni-Directional Radio Range VOR Navigation System
Very High-Frequency (VHF) Radio Communication System

Additional Keywords & Keyword Phrases for Aircraft Cargo Handling

Aircraft Cargo
Aircraft Cargo Handling
Aircraft Cargo Handling Management
Aircraft Cargo Handling Operations
Aircraft Cargo Handling Operations Management
Aircraft Cargo Loading
Aircraft Cargo Operations
Aircraft Cargo Security
Aircraft Cargo Staging
Aircraft Cargo Unloading
Baggage
Baggage Handling
Baggage Loading
Baggage Operations
Baggage Security
Baggage Staging
Baggage Unloading
Cargo
Cargo Handling
Cargo Management
Cargo Operations
Center of Gravity
Center of Gravity Computations
Ground Crew
Ground Operations
Ground Operations Management
In-Flight Cargo
In-Flight Cargo Handling
In-Flight Cargo Management
In-Flight Cargo Operations
In-Flight Cargo Security
Load Weight
Loading
Operations Management
Orientation

Transportation, Logistics, Warehousing & Distribution

Ramp Management
Ramp Operations
Ramp Operations Management
Security
Sort Operations
Sort Operations Management
Space
Space Layout
Space Management
Space Maximization
Space Optimization
Space Planning
Space Utilization
Staging
Unloading
Weight

Additional Keywords & Keyword Phrases for Airfield Operations

Aircraft
Aircraft Movement
Aircraft Status
Aircraft Status Reporting
Airfield
Airfield Construction
Airfield Ground Operations
Airfield Landing
Airfield Landing Aids
Airfield Management
Airfield Operations
Airfield Operations Management
Airfield Safety
Airfield Status
Airfield Status Reporting
Airport
Airport Construction
Airport Landing
Airport Landing Aids
Airport Management
Airport Operations
Airport Operations Management
Airport Safety
Airport Status
Airport Status Reporting
Arrival
Delays
Departures
Dispatch
Dispatch Management
Dispatch Operations
Dispatch Operations Management
Dispatching
Fuel
Fueling

Transportation, Logistics, Warehousing & Distribution

Fueling Operations
Landing
Mobile Airfield
Mobile Airfield Management
Mobile Airfield Operations
Navigation Aids
Operations
Operations Management
Passenger Loading
Passenger Services
Passenger Unloading
Refueling
Refueling Operations
Runway Construction
Runway Maintenance
Runway Repair
Takeoff

Additional Keywords & Keyword Phrases for Pilots, Copilots & Flight Engineers

Aircraft Inspection
Aircraft Operation
Aircraft Systems
Aircraft Systems Monitoring
Altitude
Attitude
Autopilot
Control Panel
Engine Operation
Engine Speed
Flight Engineering
Flight Management Computer
Flight Navigation
Flight Navigation Aids
Flight Navigation Computer
Flight Operations
Flight Operations Management
Fuel Consumption
Instrument Panel
Instrument Rating
Instruments
Multi-Engine Aircraft
Navigation
Navigational Aids
Pre-Flight Check
Pre-Flight Inspection
Radar
Single-Engine Aircraft
Steering
Twin-Engine Aircraft
Warning Devices

Additional Keywords & Keyword Phrases for Aviation Inspection

Air Navigational Aids
Aircraft Access
Aircraft Access Plate Inspection
Aircraft Door
Aircraft Door Inspection
Aircraft Door Security Inspection
Aircraft Engine
Aircraft Engine Inspection
Aircraft Fuselage
Aircraft Fuselage Inspection
Aircraft Hydraulics
Aircraft Hydraulics Inspection
Aircraft Inspection
Aircraft Landing Gear
Aircraft Landing Gear Inspection
Aircraft Maintenance
Aircraft Pneumatics
Aircraft Pneumatics Inspection
Aircraft Quality Assurance Inspection
Aircraft Quality Control Inspection
Aircraft Repair
Aircraft Systems Inspection
Aircraft Tire
Aircraft Tire Inspection
Aircraft Wing
Aircraft Wing Inspection
Airworthiness
Airworthiness Safety Inspection
Assembly Inspection
Assembly Inspector
Aviation Electrical Systems
Aviation Electronics
Aviation Electronics Systems
Aviation Hydraulics
Aviation Inspection

Aviation Maintenance Inspection
Aviation Pneumatics
Aviation Safety Inspection
Avionics Safety Inspection
Communications Equipment
Corrosion
Corrosion Inspection
Damage
Damage Inspection
Electrical Inspection
Electronics Inspection
Engine Inspection
Flight Log Inspection
Fuselage Inspection
Hydraulics
Hydraulics Inspection
Inspection
Inspection Records
Inspection Reports
Investigation
Landing Gear
Landing Gear Inspection
Maintenance Procedures Inspection
Maintenance Records Inspection
Mechanical Inspection
Pneumatics
Pneumatics Inspection
Post-Flight Inspection
Pre-Flight Inspection
Technical Inspection
Tire Inspection
Wing Inspection

Additional Keywords & Keyword Phrases for Logistics

Dedicated Logistics
Distribution
Distribution Management
Distribution Operations
Distribution Operations Management
Finished Products
Finished Products Allocation
Finished Products Availability
Finished Products Management
Integrated Logistics
Integrated Logistics Management (ILM)
Integrated Logistics Management (ILM) Management
Integrated Logistics Management (ILM) Operations
Integrated Logistics Support (ILS)
Integrated Logistics Support (ILS) Management
Integrated Logistics Support (ILS) Operations
Internal Allocation
Logistical
Logistical Operations
Logistics
Logistics Analysis
Logistics Engineering
Logistics Management
Logistics Operations
Logistics Operations Management
Logistics Performance
Logistics System
Logistics System Engineering
Materials
Materials Allocation
Materials Availability
Materials Management
Materials Operations
Materials Operations Management
Parts

Parts Allocation
Parts Availability
Parts Management
Parts Operations
Parts Operations Management
Product Acquisition
Product Distribution
Product Internal Allocation
Product Lifecycle Management
Product Management
Product Operations Management
Production
Production Operations
Production Planning
Productions Operations Management
Products
Supplies
Supply Allocation
Supply Availability
Supply Chain
Supply Chain Management
Supply Management
Warehouse Management
Warehouse Operations
Warehousing

Additional Keywords & Keyword Phrases for Maritime Transportation

Area Plotting Sheets
Barge
Bays
Beaches
Bellbook
Berth
Boat
Boiler
Buoy
Canal
Cargo
Cargo Discharging
Cargo Loading
Cargo Ship
Charter Boat
Charts
Class
Coastal Waters
Commercial Shipping
Compass
Contour Line
Course
Cruise Ship
Currents
Deck
Deck Equipment
Deck Machinery
Deep Sea
Deep-Sea Merchant Ship
Depth
Depth Finder
Depth-Finding Equipment
Depth-Finding Technology
Depth-Measuring Equipment
Depth-Measuring Technology

Docking
Dredge
Electric Motor
Electrical Systems
Electrical Systems Engineering
Electronic Sounding Device
Emergency Drill
Emergency Planning
Emergency Preparedness
Emergency Response
Engine
Engineering
Engineering Log
Estuaries
Excursion Vessel
Ferry
Ferry Boat
Flagged Ship
Foreign-Flagged Ship
Freight
Freight Ship
Gangplank
Generator
Harbor
Harbor Tug
Harbor Tugboat
Heating, Ventilating & Air Conditioning Systems (HVAC)
Heating, Ventilating & Air Conditioning Systems (HVAC) Engineering
Inland
Inland Waterways
International Organization of Masters, Mates & Pilots (IOMMP)
International Regulations
Lake
Land Sighting
Life Preserver
Lifeboat
Lifesaving Equipment
Lighthouse
Lights

Transportation, Logistics, Warehousing & Distribution

Maps
Marine Vessel Operations
Maritime
Maritime Operations
Maritime Rescue
Merchant Marines
Merchant Ship
Navigation
Navigational Aids
Navigational Guides
Navigational Systems
Ocean
Ocean Currents
Ocean Tides
Oceangoing Vessel
Passenger Cruise Ship
Passenger Discharging
Passenger Loading
Passenger Ship
Passengers
Pollution Control
Pollution Prevention
Port
Power Transmission
Propulsion
Propulsion Engine
Propulsion Engineering
Pumps
Radar
Radio Communications
Ramp
Reef
Refrigeration Systems
Refrigeration Systems Engineering
Rigging
Rivers
Sanitary Systems
Sanitary Systems Engineering
Seaport

Search & Rescue
Seas
Sewage Systems
Sewage Systems Engineering
Sextents
Ship
Ship Direction
Ship Engineering
Ship Propulsion
Ship Speed
Ship-to-Ship Communications
Ship-to-Shore Communications
Shoals
Sounds
Steering
Straits
Tanks
Tides
Tonnage
Tow Lines
Towboat
Tugboat
Unberth
US Coast Guard (USCG)
US Department of Homeland Security (DHS)
US Department of Transportation - Maritime Administration
US Merchant Marine Academy
Vessel
Vessel Class
Vessel Tonnage
Walkway
Water
Water Depth
Water Transportation
Water Vessel
Waterborne Craft
Waterways
Weather
Winches

Transportation, Logistics, Warehousing & Distribution

Wind

Additional Keywords & Keyword Phrases for Rail Transportation

Association of American Railroads (AAR)
Centralized Traffic Control Unit
Coupling
Diesel-Electric Locomotive
Electric Locomotive
Electronic Signals
Federal Railroad Administration (FRA)
Freight Locomotive
Freight Railroad
Freight Train
Gas Locomotive
Inbound
Locomotive
Locomotive Engineering
Manual Signals
Outbound
Passenger Locomotive
Passenger Railroad
Passenger Train
Rail
Rail Operations
Rail Operations Management
Rail Signaling System
Rail Switching System
Rail Terminal
Rail Traffic Track Warrant Control System
Rail Yard
Railcar
Railroad
Railroad Engineering
Railroad Regulations
Railroad Rules
Railroad Traffic Operations
Railway
Route

Transportation, Logistics, Warehousing & Distribution

Signal Control
Signals
Starting Signals
Steam Locomotive
Switch Control
Switching
Terminal
Timetable
Tower Switching Machine
Track Inspection
Tracks
Train Operations
Train Signals
Turbine Locomotive
Uncoupling
Waybill

Additional Keywords & Keyword Phrases for Trucking

Automated Routing Equipment
Automatic Loading Equipment
Automatic Loading Machinery
Auxiliary Equipment
Bills of Lading
Bulk Delivery Truck
Calibration
Cantilever Truck
Clamshell Bucket
Combination Vacuum Lift
Conveyor Belt
Counterbalanced Front Loader Lift Truck
Counterbalanced Side Loader Lift Truck
Delivery Truck
Dump Car
Electric-Powered Truck
Elevating Platform
Emergency Equipment
Flatbed Truck
Forklift
Gasoline-Powered Truck
Gauges
Gears
Gross Volume Weight (GVW)
Hand Lift
Hand Truck
High-Lift Order Picker Truck
Hitch
Hitchpin
Hoist
Hustlers
Hydraulic Lift
Inclines
Inspection
Instrument Readings

Transportation, Logistics, Warehousing & Distribution

Instruments
Interstate Transport
Interstate Transportation
Intrastate Transport
Intrastate Transportation
Johnson Bars
Lift Truck
Lift Truck Driver
Line Haul
Loading
Loading Crew
Lowboy Trailer
Lubricate
Lubrication
Maintenance
Maintenance & Repair
Man Lift
Mechanical Equipment
Merchandise Delivery
Merchandise Pick-Up
Orange Peel Bucket
Over-the-Road (OTR)
Pallet
Pallet Forklift
Personnel Lift
Platform
Platform Lift
Platform Lift Truck
Plow
Preventive Maintenance
Ramps
Reach Rider Truck
Reach-Type Outrigger Truck
Regulations
Regulatory Compliance
Rollers
Shag Truck
Skids
Sliding Boom Forklift

Sliding Tandem Axle
Straight Mast Forklift
Tilt Trailer
Tractor-Trailer
Tractor-Trailer Combination
Trailer
Trailer Hitch
Truck
Truck Lift Gates
Trucking Log
Unloading
Vehicle Log
Vehicle Maintenance
Vehicle Repair
Weight
Weight & Balance
Wheeled Loader

Additional Keywords & Keyword Phrases for Warehousing & Distribution

Automatic Loading Equipment
Automatic Loading Machinery
Cold Storage Management
Conveyor Belt
Demand Forecasting
Distribution
Distribution Management
Distribution Operations
Forklift
Hand Lift
Hand Truck
Integrated Logistics System (ILS)
Integrated Logistics System (ILS) Management
Inventory
Inventory Control
Inventory Management
Inventory Planning
Inventory Planning & Control
Load Out
Load Out Management
Loading
Loading Crew
Logistics
Logistics Management
Maintenance
Maintenance & Repair
Man Lift
Mechanical Equipment
Pallet
Pallet Forklift
Personnel Lift
Platform Lift
Preventive Maintenance
Product Management
Product Movement

Receiving
Receiving Management
Shipping
Shipping & Receiving
Shipping & Receiving Management
Shipping Management
Stockroom
Stockroom Management
Storage
Storage Management
Stores
Stores Management
Supplies
Supply Management
Warehouse
Warehouse Management
Warehouse Operations Management
Warehouse Safety
Warehouse Security

Transportation, Logistics, Warehousing & Distribution

Add Your Own Keywords & Keyword Phrases

Finding Needles in a Haystack

Chapter 15

Writing, Editing & Journalism

Principal Keyword List:

Writing, Editing & Journalism

Representative Job Titles

Advertising Copy Writer
Assignment Editor
Assistant Editor
Author
Blogger
Business Writer
Catalog Copy Writer
Copy Editor
Copy Writer
Corporate Communications Director
Corporate Communications Manager
Corporate Communications Specialist
Creative Writer
Design Editor
Desktop Publisher
Documentation Designer
Documentation Specialist
Editor
Electronic Publishing Specialist
Engineering Writer
Executive Editor
Features Editor
Internet Copy Writer
Journalist
Lyricist
Managing Editor
Manuscript Editor
Manuscript Writer
News Editor
Newspaper Copy Editor
Newspaper Reporter
Online Editor
Poet
Proofreader
Reporter
Scientific Writer

Writing, Editing & Journalism

Screenwriter
Sports Editor
Stringer
Technical Communicator
Technical Editor
Technical Writer
Vice President of Corporate Communications
Web Content Writer
Web Publications Designer
Writer

Software, Systems & Technology

Administration Software
Adobe Acrobat
Adobe Illustrator
Adobe Pagemaker
Adobe Photoshop
Corel WordPerfect
Database Query Software
Database Software
Document Management Software
FileMaker Pro
Graphic Presentation Software
Graphics Software
Hypertext Markup Language (HTML)
IBM Lotus 1-2-3
IBM Lotus Notes
Intuit QuickBooks
Macromedia Dreamweaver
Macromedia Fireworks
Macromedia Flash
Macromedia Freehand
Media Professional
Mediamix
Microsoft Access
Microsoft Excel
Microsoft Office
Microsoft Outlook
Microsoft PowerPoint
Microsoft Windows
Microsoft Word
Office Suite Software
Presentation Software
Project Management Software
Quark

Keywords & Keyword Phrases for Writing, Editing & Journalism

Search Tip: You can use the words "copy writer" and "copywriter" and "copy writing" and "copywriting" interchangeably.

Ad
Advertisement
Advertising
Advertising Brochure
Advertising Campaign
Advertising Copywriting
American Booksellers Association (ABA)
American Society of Magazine Editors (ASME)
American Society of Newspaper Editors (ASNE)
Article
Asian-American Journalists Association (AAJA)
Assembly Instructions
Associated Press (AP)
Association for Education in Journalism & Mass Communication (AEJMC)
Association of American Publishers (AAP)
Association of American University Presses (AAUP)
Association of Learned & Professional Society Publishers (ALPSP)
Audience
Audience Appeal
Blog
Blogging
Book
Book Proposal
Book Publishing
Broadcast
Broadcast Media
Brochure
Business Communications
Business Plans
Business Proposals
Business Writing
Cable Broadcast

Catalog Copywriting
Clarity
College Newspaper
Column
Commentary
Communications
Composing Room
Computer Graphics
Computer Software
Computer Technology
Computer Typesetting
Content
Content Management
Copy
Copywriting
Corporate Communications
Council of Editors of Learned Journals (CELJ)
Creative Writing
Data Analysis
Data Collection
Design
Desktop Publishing
Digital Data
Directory Publishing
Editing
Editorial
Editorial Policy
Electronic Communications
Electronic Information
Electronic Magazine (E-Zine)
Electronic Media
Electronic Newspaper
Electronic Page Layout
Electronic Publishing
English
English Grammar
English Language
English Language Syntax
Equipment Manual

Writing, Editing & Journalism

Essay
Fact Checking
Fact Finding
Feature
Feature Story
Fiction
Galley
General Interest Publication
Grammar
Graphics Design
Headline
Information
Information Analysis
Information Collection
International Publishing Management Association (IPMA)
Internet Copywriting
Internet Media
Internet Publishing
Journal Publishing
Journalism
Journalism Education Association (JEA)
Layout
Library
Library Research
Linguistics
Literary Magazine
Literary Research
Lyrics
Magazine
Magazine Publishers of America (MPA)
Magazine Publishing
Maintenance Instructions
Manuscript
Manuscript Editing
Manuscript Review
Manuscript Writing
Marketing
Marketing Brochure
Marketing Communications

Medical
Messaging
National Newspaper Association (NNA)
National Press Club (NPC)
National Scholastic Press Association (NSPA)
National Society of Newspaper Columnists (NSNC)
Newsletter
Newspaper
Newspaper Association of America (NAA)
Newspaper Reporting
Nonfiction
Novel
Operating Instructions
Order
Original Writing
Page Design
Page Layout
Periodicals Publishing
Poetry
Press Release
Print Layout
Print Media
Print Publishing
Print Space
Printers' Galley
Product Brochure
Product Literature
Product Manual
Project Management
Project Planning
Project Scheduling
Project Staffing
Promotions
Proofreading
Prop0sals
Public Announcement
Publication
Publishing
Publishing Media

Punctuation
Radio Broadcast
Readability
Reader Appeal
Readers
Reporting
Research
Research Study
Scanning
Scientific
Scientific Writing
Screenwriter
Screenwriting
Script
Short Story
Society for News Design (SND)
Society for Technical Communication (STC)
Society of Environmental Journalists (SEJ)
Society of Professional Journalists (SPJ)
Software Publishing
Speech
Spelling
Story Text
Style
Syntax
Technical
Technical Communications
Technical Documentation
Technical Editing
Technical Journals
Technical Manuals
Technical Writing
Television Broadcasting
Terminology
Text
Text Management
Tone
Trade Journal
Trade Magazine

Trade Publication
Typeset
Typography
Website Copywriting
Wire Service
Writing
Writing Style

Add Your Own Keywords & Keyword Phrases

Appendix A

Action Verbs

Following is a list of 300 action verbs that can also be used as keywords for your online recruitment searches.

Accelerate	Complete
Accomplish	Compute
Achieve	Conceive
Acquire	Conclude
Adapt	Conduct
Address	Conserve
Advance	Consolidate
Advise	Construct
Advocate	Consult
Analyze	Continue
Apply	Contract
Appoint	Convert
Arbitrate	Coordinate
Architect	Correct
Arrange	Counsel
Ascertain	Craft
Assemble	Create
Assess	Critique
Assist	Decrease
Author	Define
Authorize	Delegate
Brief	Deliver
Budget	Demonstrate
Build	Deploy
Calculate	Design
Capture	Detail
Catalog	Detect
Champion	Determine
Chart	Develop
Clarify	Devise
Classify	Direct
Close	Discover
Coach	Dispense
Collect	Display
Command	Distribute
Communicate	Diversify
Compare	Divert
Compel	Document
Compile	Double

Draft	Graduate
Drive	Guide
Earn	Halt
Edit	Head
Educate	Hire
Effect	Honor
Elect	Hypothesize
Eliminate	Identify
Emphasize	Illustrate
Enact	Imagine
Encourage	Implement
Endure	Import
Energize	Improve
Enforce	Improvise
Engineer	Increase
Enhance	Influence
Enlist	Inform
Ensure	Initiate
Establish	Innovate
Estimate	Inspect
Evaluate	Inspire
Examine	Install
Exceed	Institute
Execute	Instruct
Exhibit	Integrate
Expand	Intensify
Expedite	Interpret
Experiment	Interview
Export	Introduce
Facilitate	Invent
Finalize	Inventory
Finance	Investigate
Forge	Judge
Form	Justify
Formalize	Launch
Formulate	Lead
Found	Lecture
Generate	License
Govern	Listen

Locate	Plan
Maintain	Position
Manage	Predict
Manipulate	Prepare
Manufacture	Prescribe
Map	Present
Market	Preside
Mastermind	Process
Measure	Procure
Mediate	Program
Mentor	Progress
Model	Project
Modify	Project manage
Monitor	Promote
Motivate	Propose
Navigate	Prospect
Negotiate	Provide
Nominate	Publicize
Normalize	Purchase
Observe	Qualify
Obtain	Question
Offer	Rate
Officiate	Realign
Operate	Rebuild
Orchestrate	Recapture
Organize	Receive
Orient	Recognize
Originate	Recommend
Outsource	Reconcile
Overcome	Record
Oversee	Recruit
Participate	Redesign
Perceive	Reduce
Perfect	Reengineer
Perform	Regain
Persuade	Regulate
Pilot	Rehabilitate
Pinpoint	Reinforce
Pioneer	Rejuvenate

Render
Renegotiate
Reorganize
Report
Reposition
Represent
Research
Resolve
Respond
Restore
Restructure
Retrieve
Review
Revise
Revitalize
Satisfy
Schedule
Secure
Select
Separate
Serve
Simplify
Sold
Solidify
Solve
Specify
Speak
Standardize
Stimulate
Streamline
Structure
Succeed
Suggest
Summarize
Supervise
Supply
Support
Surpass
Synthesize

Systematize
Tabulate
Target
Teach
Terminate
Test
Thwart
Train
Transcribe
Transfer
Transform
Transition
Translate
Troubleshoot
Unify
Unite
Update
Upgrade
Use
Utilize
Verbalize
Verify
Win
Write

Appendix B

Personality Descriptors

Following is a list of 200 personality descriptors that can also be used as keywords for your online recruitment searches.

Abstract	Driven
Accurate	Dynamic
Action-Driven	Eager
Adaptable	Earnest
Adventuresome	Effective
Aggressive	Efficient
Amenable	Eloquent
Analytical	Employee-Driven
Artful	Empowered
Assertive	Encouraging
Believable	Energetic
Bilingual	Energized
Bold	Enterprising
Brave	Enthusiastic
Change Agent	Entrepreneurial
Communicative	Ethical
Competent	Experienced
Competitive	Expert
Conceptual	Expressive
Confident	Flexible
Conscientious	Forward-Thinking
Conservative	Global
Cooperative	Hardworking
Courageous	Healthy
Creative	Helpful
Credible	Heroic
Cross-Cultural	High-Impact
Culturally-Sensitive	High-Potential
Customer-Driven	Honest
Dauntless	Honorable
Decisive	Humanistic
Dedicated	Humanitarian
Dependable	Humorous
Determined	Immediate
Devoted	Important
Diligent	Impressive
Diplomatic	Incomparable
Direct	Independent
Dramatic	Individualistic

Industrious
Independent
Ingenious
Initiative
Innovative
Insightful
Intelligent
Intense
Intuitive
Judicious
Keen
Leader
Loyal
Managerial
Market-Driven
Masterful
Mature
Mechanical
Methodical
Modern
Moral
Motivated
Motivational
Multilingual
Notable
Noteworthy
Objective
Observant
Opportunistic
Oratorical
Orderly
Organized
Outstanding
Participative
Participatory
Perfectionist
Performance-Driven
Persevering
Persistent

Personable
Persuasive
Philosophical
Photogenic
Pioneering
Poised
Polished
Popular
Positive
Practical
Pragmatic
Precise
Preeminent
Prepared
Proactive
Productive
Professional
Proficient
Progressive
Prominent
Prudent
Punctual
Quality-Driven
Reactive
Reliable
Reputable
Resilient
Resourceful
Results-Driven
Results-Oriented
Savvy
Sensitive
Sharp
Skilled
Skillful
Sophisticated
Spirited
Strategic
Strong

Subjective
Successful
Tactful
Talented
Teacher
Team Builder
Team Leader
Team Player
Technical
Tenacious
Thorough
Tolerant
Top-Performer
Top-Producer
Traditional
Trainer
Trilingual
Trouble Shooter
Trustworthy
Truthful
Unrelenting
Understanding
Upbeat
Valiant
Valuable
Venturesome
Veracious
Verbal
Victorious
Vigorous
Virtuous
Visionary
Vital
Vivacious
Well-Balanced
Well-Versed
Winning
Wise
Youthful

Zealous
Zestful

Appendix C

General Skills, Qualifications & Attributes

Following is a list of 150 general skills, qualifications and attributes that can also be used as keywords for your online recruitment searches.

Accuracy	Entrepreneurial Drive
Adaptability	Entrepreneurial Vision
Analysis	Ethics
Assertiveness	Executive Leadership
Believability	Flexibility
Benchmarking	High Caliber
Best-in-Class	High Impact
Business Process Redesign	High Performance
Business Process Reengineering	Honesty
Competency	Honor
Confidence	Independence
Conflict Resolution	Inductive Reasoning
Conscientiousness	Industriousness
Cooperation	Ingeniousness
Cost Avoidance	Innovation
Cost Elimination	Intelligence
Cost Reduction	Interpersonal Relations
Courage	Integrity
Change Management	Leadership
Comprehension	Loyalty
Corporate Culture	Management
Corporate Culture Change	Maturity
Creativity	Multidisciplinary
Critical Analysis	Objectiveness
Critical Thinking	Oral Comprehension
Cross-Cultural Sensitivity	Oral Expression
Cross Functional	Organization
Cross-Functional Team Leadership	Organizational Leadership
Data Collection & Analysis	PC Proficient
Decision Making	Peak Performance
Dedication	Perfection
Deductive Reasoning	Performance Improvement
Dependability	Persistence
Devotion	Persuasiveness
Diligence	Prioritization
Diplomacy	Problem Solving
Effectiveness	Process Improvement
Efficiency Improvement	Process Redesign
Enthusiasm	Process Reengineering

Productivity Improvement
Quality Improvement
Reading Comprehension
Reliability
Resiliency
Resource Management
Resourceful
Self-Starter
Strategic
Success
Tactical
Team Building
Team Leadership
Time Management
Training & Development
World Class
Written Comprehension
Written Expression